Praise for *Enjoy Life*

Every day it seems we are bombarded with more and more *information* and *facts*, but how often do we hear someone speaking the simple *truth* to us? In her new book, Marilyn does that masterfully and powerfully, and in a way that can really help us make the changes in our lives that we need to make and that can bring us the abundant life Jesus came to give us.

I know personally what it is to be so overwhelmed by the circumstances you're facing that you lose the joy of the Lord in your life. And I know what it is to find that joy again! If you're in a situation like I found myself in several years ago, I strongly encourage you to read *Enjoy Life*. I believe the wisdom Marilyn offers from God's Word can help you learn how to enjoy life once again.

—Richard Roberts
President, Oral Roberts University
CEO & Chairman of Board of Trustees,
Oral Roberts Evangelistic Association
Co-host, "Something Good Tonight—THE HOUR OF HEALING"

Marilyn Hickey's *Enjoy Life* is a fun, refreshing perspective on the book of Ecclesiastes. Using her own life experience as the guide, Marilyn has combined wit and humor with wisdom to fine-tune our views of life, love, and happiness. It's a reminder to all of us to allow God's Word be our light so that we can truly *enjoy life!*

—Paula White
Paula White Ministries,
Without Walls International Church

Marilyn helps us to understand that God does care and have answers for everyday problems each of us face. She deciphers the many nuggets of truth given by Solomon, the wisest man that ever lived, and applies them in a practical way we can all understand. She rehearses God's continued faithfulness in her own life and helps us to understand that He is no respecter of persons. Thank you, Marilyn!

—Joni Lamb
Daystar Television Network

Marilyn Hickey, the only person I know who could write a book on fasting and make you look forward to doing it, has now written a book on Ecclesiastes—and makes that book look cheerful, exciting, and easy to understand. What an amazing gift she has! You won't be able to put it down!'

—R.T. Kendall
RT Kendall Ministries

Jesus came that we might have life and might have it more abundantly, and He wants us to enjoy every single minute of the day and night! Marilyn Hickey has put together a book that will astound you because it is taken from the book of Ecclesiastes. The wonderful revelation she had will make you wish you were a speed reader because you can't wait to get to the next page.

—Frances Hunter
Hunter Ministries

· enjoy life ·

moving past everyday struggles

marilyn hickey

NELSON BOOKS
A Division of Thomas Nelson Publishers
Since 1798

www.thomasnelson.com

Copyright © 2006 by Marilyn Hickey

Published in Nashville, Tennessee, by Thomas Nelson, Inc.
www.thomasnelson.com

Nelson Books titles may be purchased in bulk for educational, business, fund-raising, or sales promotional use. For information, please e-mail
SpecialMarkets@ThomasNelson.com.

Unless otherwise stated, all Scripture passages are from The Message (MSG), copyright ©1993. Used by permission of NavPress Publishing Group. Other Scripture references are from the following sources: The New King James Version (NKJV®), copyright 1979, 1980, 1982, Thomas Nelson, Inc., Publishers. The King James Version of the Bible (KJV). The Holy Bible, New International Version (NIV), copyright ©1973, 1978, 1984, International Bible Society. Used by permission of Zondervan Bible Publishers. New Living Translation (NLT) Holy Bible. New Living Translation copyright © 1996 by Tyndale Charitable Trust. Used by permission of Tyndale House Publishers.

Enjoy Life!
Marilyn Hickey Ministries
P.O. Box 6598
Englewood, CO 80155-6598
mhmin.org

ISBN: 1–5955–1005–7

Library of Congress Cataloging-in-Publication Data

Hickey, Marilyn.
  Enjoy life! : moving past everyday struggles / Marilyn Hickey.
    p. cm.
  Includes bibliographical references and index.
  ISBN 1-59951-005-7 (alk. paper)
  1. Bible. O.T. Ecclesiastes—Criticism, interpretation, etc. 2. Contentment—Biblical teaching. I. Title.
  BS1475.52.H53 2006
  223'.806—dc22

2006015011

Printed in the United States of America
1 2 3 4 5 6 — 09 08 07 06

contents

chapter 1

enjoying life isn't a sin

Have you ever thought, *What is life really all about? Is this all there is?* You wonder why you work so hard, just to get up and do it again tomorrow. Life feels dark.

There was a time when my life felt that way.

I had traveled and preached for a living. Studying the Word of God, as well as talking and praying with people, was my livelihood and my lifestyle. But through my travels, I contracted a debilitating illness.

No one knew what was wrong. I endured many medical tests, but none of them delivered a diagnosis. The doctors said, "Maybe it's your heart." They confined me to the hospital for two days, ran more tests, then announced, "You have the heart of a forty-year-old." Great news to a seventy-two-year-old! But still, no diagnosis.

Food lost its taste, so I lost my appetite along with twenty pounds. I looked like a bag of bones. I shook all the time on the inside. People's voices jarred me to no end; as a result, I would go to church late and leave early to avoid conversation. Too weak to drive my car, too sick to fly in an airplane, I was forced to cancel all travel plans. I fell into depression; as my body deteriorated, my mind declined, too. I had just finished memorizing the book of John, but to my dismay, I couldn't recall any of it! And then not to know what was wrong with me . . .

As I lay in bed, the enemy pestered my mind with thoughts like "You're dying. You'll never preach again. You had that big crusade in Pakistan, but you'll never have another."

However, the Lord helped me by doing something extraordinary. He led me to read Ecclesiastes, the gloomiest book in the Bible! Even though I had read the entire Bible many times over, I had *never* enjoyed reading this book. So negative!

Yet this time, as I began to read the first chapter, I discovered that the writer described exactly how I felt: "Meaningless! Meaningless! . . . Everything is meaningless" (Eccles. 1:2 NIV). As I continued reading through the most pessimistic pages in the Word of God, an amazing thing happened! *The Lord began to show me how to enjoy life.*

Who would have thought that during the most negative time in my life, reading the most negative book in the Bible, He would show me a truth so simple, yet so profound: God wants you and me to enjoy our lives!

Eventually, the doctors reached a diagnosis and my health was restored. Although I was ill for seven months, I was delighted at the end by a double transformation—good health and happiness.

What do you do when your life feels dark? When you feel as if . . .

   . . . you can't live with your husband.
   . . . you don't like your kids.
   . . . you can't stand your boss.

Instead of feeling frustrated and hopeless, what would it be like to enjoy life? The ability to enjoy your life is a gift from God! And He wants to show you how.

chapter 2

are you bored?

Growing up, the mind-set in my parents' German home was to work very hard, be extremely disciplined, and learn to provide for yourself. Consequently, I have always worked exceptionally hard and pushed myself to accomplish. When I wanted to pursue a college education, my dad's comment was, "Great, but I'm not paying for it. Get scholarships and work your way through." So that's what I did.

All of my life I was taught: achieve, discipline myself, achieve, discipline myself. Therefore, I carried that mind-set into my spiritual life. Frankly, I subconsciously thought it was a sin to enjoy life.

But God changed the way I think. Lying sick in bed feeling deathly ill, I couldn't accomplish anything. I felt trapped! I felt bored out of my mind! The devil told me I was losing my mind, but the Lord gave me a mental and spiritual revelation.

4

Do you feel trapped inside your present circumstances? Are you bored with your life? Are you tired of
the same old problems, the same old things, the same old
crises? Are you thinking, *I just want to stop the world and
get off!*?

Well, don't stop the world and get off. Inspired by the
Spirit of God, the writer of Ecclesiastes, King Solomon,
describes a life view. Does it match yours?

There's nothing to anything—it's all smoke.
What's there to show for a lifetime of work,
a lifetime of working your fingers to the bone?
One generation goes its way, the next one arrives,
but nothing changes—it's business as usual for old
    planet earth.
The sun comes up and the sun goes down,
then does it again, and again—the same old round.
The wind blows south, the wind blows north.
Around and around and around it blows,
blowing this way, then that—the whirling, erratic
    wind.
All the rivers flow into the sea,
but the sea never fills up.
The rivers keep flowing to the same old place,
and then start all over and do it again.
Everything's boring, utterly boring—
no one can find any meaning in it.

Boring to the eye,
boring to the ear.
What was will be again,
what happened will happen again.
There's nothing new on this earth.
Year after year it's the same old thing.
Does someone call out, "Hey, this is new"?
Don't get excited—it's the same old story.
Nobody remembers what happened yesterday.
And the things that will happen tomorrow?
Nobody'll remember them either.
Don't count on being remembered.

—*Ecclesiastes 1:2–11*

Do you view life this way?

"I have seen all the works that are done under the sun; and indeed, all is *vanity*..." (Eccles. 1:14 NKJV, emphasis mine). Throughout the twelve chapters of Ecclesiastes, Solomon refers to life "under the sun" twenty-nine times and describes this life as "vanity" meaning "meaningless" thirty-seven times (KJV).

King Solomon is describing an "under-the-sun" life view. God, however, has something much better for you, and it's so enjoyable! It's life "under the Son."

"Under-the-sun" living views life from a secular, horizontal standpoint, noticing people and the surrounding environment.

"Under-the-Son" living views life vertically, looking upward to God. It's *asking*, "Jesus, will You come into my dark situation? I need Your light to show me what to do." It's *trusting* God to take your situation and do something good. It's *watching* for the answer. It's *noticing* what He does and *thanking* Him for it, even all the little things that make you feel good in your daily existence. It's *believing* He makes all things beautiful as you walk through the seasons of your life. And ultimately, it's *looking forward* to enjoying heaven.

Living life from an under-the-Son viewpoint is living a life of faith, not a life of negativity. Basically, the word faith means trusting God to take a situation and do something good. Viewing life this way, no matter what you're feeling or going through, ensures *you won't have a boring life*.

When I began to read Ecclesiastes, I was at a point in my life where I was sick and I thought, *Everything's dull, everything's a drag. I've done it all.* Nothing was new and exciting anymore. I felt like I didn't have anything to look forward to. My negative thoughts pulled down my emotions until I felt passionless about life.

From deep within I cried, *I feel terrible! I'm not hungry enough to eat. When I drink my morning cup of coffee, it tastes horrid! God, where are You?* I felt like Solomon's description of the person who lives under the sun crying out, "Life is meaningless!"

If ever there lived a person who had the opportunity and inclination to discover what gives life its meaning, it was King Solomon. Born around 990 B.C., his reign as king of Israel began when he was about twenty years old. He reigned until his death at approximately 930 B.C. The richest king ever to rule Israel lists his annual income as 666 talents of gold, which is roughly equivalent to $20 million today, and that didn't include income from traveling merchants, traders, kings of Arabia, and governors of the country (see 1 Kings 10:14–15 NKJV). Ruling during peacetime in Israel, he had the time, wealth, and human resources at his command to investigate the meaning of life. During the latter part of his reign, he wrote the practical book of Ecclesiastes, covering every aspect of life from birth to death.

Throughout Ecclesiastes, King Solomon takes us on a tour of life, revealing the emptiness of an under-the-sun lifestyle, while threading the hope of an enjoyable under-the-Son lifestyle.

Why did he write it? He wanted to record his pursuit of the meaning of life to save us the time and money, and to prevent us from making his mistakes. Instead, he wanted us to enjoy every day of our lives.

Are you ready to find out what Solomon discovered?

The first thing Solomon tried was the pursuit of knowledge:

I looked most carefully into everything, searched
out all that is done on this earth.

—*Ecclesiastes 1:13*

Have you ever thought, *My life is boring. I think I'll go
back to school and get my degree?* After a while, Solomon
had studied enough to acknowledge:

I know more and I'm wiser than anyone before me in
Jerusalem. I've stockpiled wisdom and knowledge.

—*Ecclesiastes 1:16*

Did it satisfy him? His surprising conclusion:

The more you know, the more you hurt.

—*Ecclesiastes 1:18*

The more you learn, the more you realize how igno-
rant you still are. More knowledge doesn't fill the empty
feeling inside.

Next, Solomon thought, *I'll test pleasure to see if it
gives meaning to my life.* Have you ever decided to throw
away all your cares and just do whatever feels good?
Solomon did. Determined to have fun, he experimented
with a profuse amount of sexual partners.

I said to myself, "Let's go for it—experiment with pleasure, have a good time!"

—*Ecclesiastes 2:1*

His deduction?

What do I think of the fun-filled life? Insane!
    Inane!
My verdict on the pursuit of happiness? Who needs it?
With the help of a bottle of wine
and all the wisdom I could muster,
I tried my level best
to penetrate the absurdity of life.
I wanted to get a handle on anything useful we
    mortals might do
during the years we spend on this earth.

—*Ecclesiastes 2:2–3*

You know, when you look at life under the sun as Solomon did, it feels sour. Do you know why? It's because you're looking at life from a horizontal viewpoint, blind to anything supernatural. Oh, I tell you, when people don't have God, life is so empty, or when people have God in their lives but don't notice what He's doing for them daily.

So full of what we see on television and read in news-papers, our minds have become diverted from noticing God. We don't give ourselves an opportunity to know there is a God or to acknowledge what He is doing for us.

But there is a one true God, and He is working on your behalf! Life in the Son transforms life under the sun, helping you enjoy all of life. Instead of life that's dead and a drag, life is fun! I'm having more fun now than ever be-fore because I've learned that God gives wonderful enjoy-ment of life for every one of us. It's His gift.

When my health began to return, I woke up one morning and was overjoyed to discover I could taste my coffee. I had never thought about how great it tasted un-til that moment. All of a sudden, it dawned on me to thank the Lord for the ability to enjoy it. It was a gift from Him to me.

Solomon eventually discovered joy in life, too, but before he did, what else did he try? After he failed to find the meaning of life through the pursuit of pleasure, Solomon decided to try the opposite. He threw himself into working hard, wholeheartedly laboring to build and create all he could:

Oh, I did great things:
built houses,
planted vineyards,

designed gardens and parks
and planted a variety of fruit trees in them,
made pools of water
to irrigate the groves of trees.

—*Ecclesiastes 2:4–6*

Have you ever thought, *Maybe I'll be happier if I work a lot?* And so you dive in and work, work, work. Just like Solomon, you think, *I'll achieve. I'll create. I'll accomplish something new.* In my line of work, I could think, *I'll go on more Christian television shows than any woman in the world. I'll travel to more countries.*

But you know, unless your work is directed by the Son, it becomes just another part of living life under the sun. Just like my coffee when I was sick, life becomes tasteless. As you wonder, *What's wrong with me? What's going on?* God is saying, *Would you just stop and let Me be in charge? Would you enjoy what I have given you? Would you enjoy your grandchildren? Would you just enjoy putting your feet up and marveling at the sunset I made for you?*

I live in Colorado in a house with a huge picture window that frames some pine trees outdoors. Do you know, I lived in this lovely house for about four years before I enjoyed the view! I never enjoyed it until I got so sick all I could do was lie down and look out the window. I realized I'd been missing out on God's gift to me.

Completely bored, Solomon next tried collecting things. Oh, how he collected—male and female slaves, silver and gold, singers and women. First Kings 11:3 records the astonishing fact that Solomon had "seven hundred royal wives and three hundred concubines."

Do you collect? *I don't feel satisfied, so I think I'll buy a Bentley and a Porsche. I'll own the most houses. I'll have the most mink coats. I'll possess the most beautiful clothes. I'll own as many shoes as Imelda Marcos.*

Collect, collect, collect. But you see, collecting doesn't satisfy:

I hated everything I'd accomplished and accumulated on this earth.

—*Ecclesiastes 2:18*

Why? He says he took a good look at everything he'd sweated and worked for only to realize he would have to leave it all behind when he died (and to people who might not appreciate or take care of it). Therefore, everything he'd worked for was worthless. He said it was as if he'd simply spit into the wind.

Everything he learned, indulged in, created, and collected was as worthless as smoke. In his pursuit for the meaning of life under the sun, he concluded:

It's all smoke, nothing but smoke. The smart and
    the stupid both disappear out of sight.
In a day or two they're both forgotten. Yes, both the
    smart and the stupid die, and that's it.
I hate life. As far as I can see, what happens on
    earth is a bad business. It's smoke—
and spitting into the wind.

—Ecclesiastes 2:15–17

Are you bored? Do you hate your life? Since Solomon has already figured out that learning more, pursuing pleasure, working longer hours, and amassing things doesn't alleviate the empty feeling inside, we would waste our time, resources, and money following in his footsteps. We can learn from the conclusions he drew and decide not to look at our lives from a disillusioned, under-the-sun viewpoint.

Instead, we can look up and say, "Oh, Jesus, reveal Yourself to me. If there really is a God up there, and if You really love me, I want to know You." If you already have a relationship with Jesus, you can say, "Jesus, I want to know You more! I want to enjoy this life You've given me."

He'll do it. He'll reveal Himself to you because "This is how much God loved the world: He gave his Son, his one and only Son. And this is why: so that no one need be destroyed; by believing in him, anyone can have a whole and lasting life" (John 3:16). Life lived apart from Jesus is temporary, like smoke. Here for a minute, then gone.

But Jesus gives you eternal life. Not only that, but He has a plan for all of our lives that is beyond what we can imagine or expect: "It's in Christ that we find out who we are and what we are living for. Long before we first heard of Christ and got our hopes up, he had his eye on us, had designs on us for glorious living, part of the overall purpose he is working out in everything and everyone" (Eph. 1:11–12).

I know about God's goodness from firsthand experience. One day during my illness when I was lying in bed, completely bored, and so weak I could barely walk across a room, something wonderful happened. As I was sleeping, the Lord gave me a dream.

I saw myself in Europe just as the sun was rising. I was in a city, walking up the hill of a city street! In my dream, I thought, *I'm healthy. I'm walking up a hill. I have energy!* And then I thought, *I'm in Europe. I have to call our executive director of global events and say, "Have lunch with me. I'm ready to have a meeting."* Then the dream was over.

At that point, I knew the Son had spoken to me! He filled me with hope. I was experiencing life under the

Son instead of life under the sun! And do you know, about a year and a half after I recovered, my daughter and I were holding a meeting in Naples, Italy. When we arrived in the busy downtown area, I noticed a street that looked familiar. I had never been in this part of Naples in all my life, but I found myself thinking, *Why does this street look so familiar?* Then it hit me—this was the very street with the hill I had walked up in my dream! The sun was coming up, and I was able to walk, just as in the dream.

That kind of living, connected to a God who loves you and fills you with hope, is life under the Son. It's supernatural living.

Are you living life under the Son? Or do you realize you've been trying everything Solomon tried in his search for meaning, only to discover, as he did, that you're still not fulfilled in life?

Do you think God is mad at you? When you can't get anything done, do you believe He doesn't love you as much as when you're running around accomplishing all your goals? Do you think He doesn't want you to enjoy what you eat and drink? Do you think work is merely a necessary part of life, and that God couldn't possibly want you to enjoy what you accomplish?

If this mind-set is accurate, then why does Ecclesiastes 2:24 say, "Nothing is better for a man than that he should eat and drink, and that his soul should enjoy good in his labor. This also, I saw, was from the hand of God" (NKJV)? Several times, the book of Ecclesiastes says He gives you the gift of enjoying life, the gift of eating, and drinking, and being joyful.

Enjoyment is from the hand of God—it's His idea! God wants you to enjoy life!

He wants you to take a look at what you've accomplished and enjoy it! That could mean stepping back after you finish a project at work or school and thinking, *I did it! Lord, thank You.* Or observing your house after you've cleaned it and admitting, *I did a good job! This looks good! Thank You, Lord.*

Instead of imagining the worst about God, it's wise to look into His Word and acknowledge the truth—life is a gift from God and He gives us the ability to enjoy it.

A big part of the problem in living life under the sun is that we are me-oriented: "I didn't like this meal—the pizza wasn't as good as usual." Or "My wife didn't say good morning to me today. Then she turned my eggs over and fried them just the way I *don't* like them." Or "My son doesn't remember to take the trash out on his own." Or "I didn't get much out of church yesterday."

That's the "me life." Me, me, me. I, I, I. If you go through and count all of the "I's" in chapter 1 and 2 of Ecclesiastes, you'll be astounded.

Is that where you are? Could the cause of your boredom be that you're me-centered instead of Christ-centered? The hope Solomon threads through Ecclesiastes is his discovery that God is your source for meaning and enjoyment of life.

What do you do when your life feels meaningless? God has something so good for you, you can't even imagine how good it is! I tell you, we feel empty many times in life because we don't notice what God is giving us or we don't believe in God, who made us and who has created a destiny for us beyond anything we can imagine or expect. Oh, He is so good to us!

Are you noticing and thanking Him for the little things He gives you each day? Life under the Son is better than you could ever dream it to be. "I came so they can have real and eternal life, more and better life than they ever dreamed of" (John 10:10). Then you'll be able to say, "Not only am I alive, but I enjoy my life! And I'm looking forward to spending eternity with Jesus."

From the moment I began to understand that life is enjoyable in the Son, let me tell you, I decided that I would say first thing when I wake up every morning, "Lord, thank You for this day. This is the best day of my life! It's a gift from You; may I spend it well."

Life is fragile. You and I don't know how long we have here on earth. Even in the most ordinary, daily circumstances of our lives, let's acknowledge that Christ has given us life and let's enjoy the work of our hands, the food, and the beverages He has given us. He is so wonderful!

What a great day when the doctors found out I was afflicted with parasites—bad news, but I had a diagnosis! I had traveled to a country called Kazakhstan, and I think there's where I probably picked them up. Until that time, I had been so busy pushing myself to get things done, reading the Bible, memorizing Scripture, calling people, ministering to people, and taping TV shows, that I had never taken time to enjoy life. When this realization struck me, I said, "*God, I didn't realize You've given me things to warm my life, things for me to enjoy. To enjoy food is a gift from You! To enjoy my coffee is a gift from You! To enjoy special things. Thank You!*"

You see, I hadn't taken time to notice God's enjoyable gifts because I was such a disciplined, high achiever. I don't believe God made me sick; I believe the devil made me sick. But God is so good. During this time of grave illness, He not only healed me physically, but He transformed me mentally.

I have a new mind-set, and God wants you to have it, too: It's OK to enjoy your life! *God wants you to!*

chapter 3

enjoying the seasons of life

How can you enjoy life when you're going through a hard time?

When my daughter, Sarah, started school, I struggled with my emotions. I thought, *Oh, she's not my baby anymore. She's gone.* Then she grew older, entered junior high and said, "Mom and Dad, I don't need you to come into my room to say good night anymore," and she would close her bedroom door. We would still pray with her, but she didn't want us to come into her room. I struggled with feelings of being shut out of her life. My husband and I had to adjust.

It was a season of life.

Then Sarah went away to Oral Roberts University. I was accustomed to taking care of her every day, and then suddenly, she was gone. One day, I walked into her room and burst into tears.

The Lord said to me, "Well, what do you want?"

"I want her to do Your will," I replied.

He asked, "Is it My will for her to go to Oral Roberts University?"

I knew it was, so I responded, "Yes."

He responded, "Well, she is doing My will. So what are you crying about?"

I quit crying! God helped me enjoy this new season.

Later on, when Sarah married, my husband and I became in-laws. When she and her husband had children, my husband and I became grandparents. In each season, we learned to adjust. We learned to place each new season in God's hands.

We all go through seasons in life.

As part of Solomon's tour of life, he discloses the seasons we can expect to go through during the course of our lives. "To everything *there is* a season, A time for every purpose under heaven" (Eccles. 3:1 NKJV):

A right time for birth and another for death,
A right time to plant and another to reap,
A right time to kill and another to heal,
A right time to destroy and another to construct,
A right time to cry and another to laugh,
A right time to lament and another to cheer,
A right time to make love and another to abstain,

A right time to embrace and another to part,
A right time to search and another to count your
losses,
A right time to hold on and another to let go,
A right time to rip out and another to mend,
A right time to shut up and another to speak up,
A right time to love and another to hate,
A right time to wage war and another to make
peace.

—*Ecclesiastes 3:2–8*

This is the whole panorama of life—God lets you in on the whole ball game. If you read this when you're young, it's a great sneak preview! Don't get depressed because you interpret it from the wrong viewpoint.

So what is God's viewpoint? Throughout your lifetime, you will encounter a range of activities that are shared by all human beings. Your life will consist of a mixture of conflicting experiences. Every day isn't going to be "Oh happy day!" Instead, God says there will be a time to cry and a time to laugh. You won't spend all of your time crying, but neither will you spend all of your time laughing.

When you experience these seasons, don't think you're abnormal. God inspired Solomon to write this down so you wouldn't feel strange when you find yourself going through these times in your life. God wants you to experience what He will do for you when you choose to live life under the Son, bringing Jesus into every season.

God wants to help by transforming your attitudes and turning around your negative circumstances. "Hour by hour I place my days in your hand, safe from the hands out to get me" (Ps. 31:15). Are you willing to place every season and its circumstances in God's hands?

Let's investigate these seasons.

First, in verse 2, Solomon lists the *most momentous seasons of your life*: birth and death. We were all born into this world, and unless the Second Coming of Jesus occurs in our lifetime, we will all die.

The next three seasons in verses 2 and 3 deal with *creative and destructive human activities:* (1) planting and reaping, (2) killing and healing, and (3) destroying and constructing. The verbs used here—plant, reap, kill, heal, destroy, and construct—describe specific human activities as well as all of our creative and destructive, good and evil, pursuits in life. You'll go through productive times in life, such as planting time and harvest time. But interspersed with these will be times when you stop to pull the weeds and clean up the dried tomato plants.

Where did people get the idea that everything in life is sweet and ideal forever? It's not. You'll live through times of creative and destructive human activities.

After this, Solomon lists two pairs of *human emotions*. We think, *Oh, I just want my emotions to be stable all the time*. Well, I wish I could say mine always have been, are now, and always will be! Instead, verse 4 says there is (1) a time to cry and a time to laugh and (2) a time to lament and a time to cheer.

Folks, there are going to be times when you're going to dance and celebrate, but there are going to be times when you're going to mourn over someone, too. This is life, and everyone who has ever been born on this earth goes through these seasons.

But that's not all. The next two seasons of life listed in verse 5 deal with *relationships*: (1) a time to make love and a time to abstain and (2) a time to embrace and a time to part.

Parents experience times when their children beg for affection in place of correction. They don't want you to be direct and honest with them about their behavior. "Oh, hug me, Mother," they'll plead. But the time isn't right to hug them; the time is right to correct them or tell them "This is wrong. This is not the right thing to do." In life, we'll experience unpleasant times when it isn't the appropriate time to embrace. There will be times in life like these when things aren't all lovey-dovey.

After my husband had knee replacement surgery, it was hard for him to go through the doctor-recommended

steps to get well. His physical therapist told him to exercise and stop using his crutches, but he didn't.

So we called a family meeting. Four of us—our son
Michael, our daughter Sarah, our daughter's husband
Reece, and I—met with my husband, Wally. Reece reit-
erated the doctor's instructions along with the consequences if my husband didn't follow them. He reminded
my husband that the doctor had stated, "If you don't do
these things, at the end of twelve months, you won't be
any better." The rest of us chimed in, reminding my husband of his desire to walk three miles a day as he had before the surgery. We explained to him that we were only
trying to help him because we're family and we love him.

When everybody left, my husband fumed, "I don't
like family meetings! It's just family-bashing time, and
everybody bashes on *me*." Oh, was he upset!

So I reminded him, "Why did everybody talk to you?"

"Well, because they love me," he admitted.

I continued, "Well, did we advise you to do things
that made good sense or bad sense?"

"Well, good sense."

"Did the doctor say to do them?"

"Yes."

The next morning, he got up from bed without using
the crutches. What's more, he was smiling and happy!
He never picked up the crutches again.

But you see, this was a time not to embrace. We couldn't just hug him and say, "Oh, Dad, are you better? We're here for you." Everyone had been there for him all along, but he needed a point in time where we refrained from embracing him and were direct with him instead. We all need seasons of correction. They're good for us and are simply part of the seasons of life.

The next two seasons address our *possessions*: (1) A time to search and a time to count your losses, and (2) "A time to hold on and a time to let go." As you walk through life, there are times when things come in, but there are times when you need to get them out. For example, when you notice you have too much in your house, you clean out the cupboards and give your possessions to people who need them.

I try to clean out my closet once a year. We all have clothes we don't wear but hold on to so long they finally go out of style. I've learned when something doesn't fit me anymore to give it away. We need to give things away to keep a flow of giving and receiving in our lives. Who wants to become like the Dead Sea where everything comes in and nothing goes out!

Gaining and losing, keeping and throwing away are seasons of reorganizing. Solomon tells us they are just a part of life.

The last four seasons Solomon discloses are: (1) A time

to rip out and a time to mend, (2) A time to shut up and a time to speak up, (3) A time to love and a time to hate, and (4) A time to wage war and a time to make peace.

Ripping out and mending may refer to times of repenting for sin and receiving forgiveness: "'Don't tear your clothing in your grief; instead, tear your hearts.' Return to the LORD your God, for he is gracious and merciful" (Joel 2:13 NLT).

Next, there's a time to talk and not to talk. Folks, may I say it? Sometimes God just wants you to shut up. There are times when I know I shouldn't say anything. There are times when a situation is none of our business and we shouldn't give our opinion. However, there are times when it is the right time to speak up. Some of those times, God will even tell you exactly what to say.

There's a time to love, but there's something God instructs us to hate: God hates sin and we must hate it, too. We want everyone to be saved from hell, but the Bible informs us there's a narrow gate going to heaven and a broad gate going to hell (Matt. 7:13–14). You and I don't like it that way—if we'd written the Bible, we wouldn't have put that in there but that's what it says. The Lord is so full of love that "He wants . . . everyone saved" (1 Tim. 2:4), but not all people will ask Jesus to be their Savior and go to heaven. We cannot compromise on this truth. We must love the sinner but hate his sin.

Last, there are seasons of wartime and peacetime. Nations engage in national war and peaceful endeavors, and in everyday civilian life, we experience trials and victories, ups and downs. These times are all part of life.

Now here's the most important point Solomon makes about the seasons—oh, you're going to love this! It will help you so much!

God made everything beautiful in itself and in its time . . . .

—*Ecclesiastes 3:11*

Do you understand what He is saying to you? In whatever season you're in, if you will ask Him, God will make it beautiful.

Oh, in the worst situation, if you'll allow Him, He will come into it. Put your times in His hand! Ask Jesus to come into your season and turn around the negative circumstances for His glory. He wants to make everything beautiful. He can bring something good out of everything you're involved in at this moment.

Instead of battling and beating against the season you find yourself in, tormenting yourself emotionally and mentally, asking yourself why life is so hard, invite God into it. He will bring satisfaction. He will bring the blessing that He alone can give in each season of your life.

You may protest, "If God is so good, why does He allow suicide bombers to walk into a hotel and blow up fifty-six people? Why does He allow catastrophes like tsunamis? Why does He allow children to starve? *Doesn't God care?*"

In this world, there exists a real devil who influences people to commit terrible crimes. God is not unaware. He loves everyone.

Judgment will come. God has a perfect time for this, too. Solomon writes:

> I said to myself, "God will judge righteous and wicked." There's a right time for every thing, every deed—and there's no getting around it.

> —*Ecclesiastes 3:17*

Not only do we have the hope of impending judgment to hold on to, but here's a key to help ease your mind: Look for God's turnarounds during times of disaster.

After the tsunami in Bande Ache, Indonesia, where thousands of people died within ten minutes, I traveled there to help. So many people died, they had to be buried in the earth in seven layers because there wasn't enough space to spread them out in separate burial plots. Such a tragedy!

But here are some good things God did. Up until that time, Indonesia had never allowed a Christian entrance into that area of its country.

When a crisis hits and you're starving, whoever brings the food is the person you're going to accept it from, whether they're a Muslim or a Christian or a Buddhist or anything else.

When this crisis hit, who showed up first? Christians! Where were the Africans who had been selling them arms? Nowhere to be found. When the Acehinese needed food, Christians leaped to the rescue.

As a result, the whole community is now awakening to the Gospel.

Yes, that was an awful tragedy, but did God do something good in the middle of it? Yes, He did! And He can do something beautiful in your situation, in the negative circumstance you're enduring. He did in mine.

When I went through the hardest season I've ever lived through, the seven months when I was extremely ill with parasites, I asked God for help. Then a doctor said to me, "Marilyn, go spend time with your grandchildren. Forget everything else. You're running around the world trying to save it, but God can save the world without you. Why don't you just go enjoy your grandchildren?"

Even though I didn't feel well and didn't have much

energy, I took the doctor's advice. I would go over to Sarah's house and bathe her three little children. As I did, I added something I love to do—I told Bible stories. Their favorite became the story of Naaman who was healed from leprosy by dipping in the water seven times. We enjoyed our time together, and I can't tell you the therapy it was for me! Even though it was physically strenuous, it helped me on the inside.

There was another way God made that hard season of my life beautiful. Inviting God into this season changed me from being me-focused (Oh, I feel so bad today) to being Christ-focused (How can I help someone else feel better today?). Life under the Son simply is that way because Jesus has a giving nature. The same God who gave Himself up to death on the cross for us now wants to live inside us and keep on giving through us.

As a result, the Lord led me to call six people a day to pray with and encourage. I would think, *I feel worse than they do*. But I did it because I didn't want to be so focused on me, viewing life from an under-the-sun perspective instead of from under the Son! The Lord gave me the desire to think His giving thoughts instead of pessimistic me-centered thoughts. I can't tell you how much the act of encouraging other people encouraged me! I needed to reach out and help other people in order to find God's blessing and beauty in that season of my life. Through giving, I experienced enjoyment when I was going through a hard time.

When we think about all of the seasons of life, it causes us to ask ourselves, *What season am I in right now? Do I want God to transform it from just plain ugly to beautiful? When I've blown it—when I've said or done something wrong—do I go to Him and ask Him to make it beautiful?*

I remember the day when I decided to help my teenage daughter, Sarah, clean out her car. When I opened the car door, a beer can rolled out onto the ground. Heartbroken, I started to cry.

Sarah stood there watching, summoning up the courage to explain. "Mom, you never listen to me when I try to talk to you. You always preach to me."

You know, in the middle of that grievous moment, God opened my heart and mind to understand how wrong I'd been. I turned around that day in my relationship with my daughter, listening instead of preaching. God made our relationship beautiful.

chapter 4

stop struggling

Are you struggling in your relationships with family, friends, or coworkers? We all need transformation in this area. If we ask Jesus to help our relationships, He will.

I like how Solomon tells the truth about relationships. He explores the meaning of life, the seasons we all live through, and our relationships head-on. He isn't afraid to ask searching questions that plague us all.

First, he examines the relationships we have with people in power over us. How many times have we witnessed corrupt political leaders squandering their country's resources on themselves?

Then I returned and considered all the oppression that is done under the sun:

Next I turned my attention to all the outrageous violence that takes place on this planet—the tears of the victims, no one to comfort them; the iron grip of oppressors, no one to rescue the victims from them. So I congratulated the dead who are already dead instead of the living who are still alive. But luckier than the dead or the living is the person who has never even been, who has never seen the bad business that takes place on this earth.

—*Ecclesiastes 4:1–3*

Life without God can be depressing. But when we ask God to transform specific adverse situations, He does!

I traveled to Romania in 1989 to preach in the underground church. At midnight, my group was stopped at the border and questioned. We stood out in the cold for about an hour while the patrol searched our car and luggage. If they found a Bible on us, they would prevent our entry into the country. Finally we were cleared, so we got back in the car and drove for a day to reach our destination.

At that time, Nicolae Ceausescu was the leader of Communist Romania. We could see billboards with Ceausescu's picture boldly displayed in public places as we secretly traveled to the underground church. The signs read "Ceausescu, our hero."

Well, he wasn't a hero. He was a thug. During the coldest time of the year, he ordered the heat turned off in the hospitals. Ten thousand babies died! He didn't care; he did it on purpose.

When I saw those signs, I began to pray, "God, take this evil man out of power. Please, take him out of control!" His cruelty lit such a fire in me that when I returned to the United States, I implored congregations all over America to ask God to remove him from power within that year.

In December, the news reported an uprising in Romania. Nicolae and his wife, Elena, had fled. I prayed, "Lord, let the authorities find them." The police captured them and turned them over to the army. They were condemned to death for their crimes and executed on December 25, 1989. Afterward, Romania became a democratic government.

When we live on a horizontal level, life is depressing, just as Solomon described it, but when we choose to live under the Son and ask God to help us, He does!

Next, Solomon reveals how our work ethic affects our relationships with family and friends:

Then I observed all the work and ambition motivated by envy. What a waste! Smoke. And spitting into the wind.

The fool sits back and takes it easy,
His sloth is slow suicide.

One handful of peaceful repose
Is better than two fistfuls of worried work—
More spitting into the wind.

I turned my head and saw yet another wisp of
smoke on its way to nothingness: a solitary person, completely alone—no children, no family,
no friends—yet working obsessively late into the
night, compulsively greedy for more and more,
never bothering to ask, "Why am I working like a
dog, never having any fun? And who cares?"
More smoke. A bad business.

—*Ecclesiastes 4:4–8*

Here Solomon sees human rivalry (envy) as the
main motivation behind our rat race for wealth, status,
and power. Too easily, we overwork ourselves (two fistfuls). He contrasts overworking and laziness in an effort to reveal God's happy medium (one handful). The
person who asks God for His wisdom will attempt a lot
(one handful) but not too much (two fistfuls). Working this way will spare him from the nerve-wracking
"spitting-into-the-wind" strain of working life.

You know, there's an overachiever out there over-working himself, but nobody likes him. Why? No one knows him. He's a lonely man, working such long hours he eliminates companionship from his life.

Perhaps he doesn't go home. Or if he goes home, it's late. If he has a family, he doesn't spend time with them. He never takes time to rest and be refreshed. He's work-ing harder than God intended him to work. *Two fistfuls of worried work instead of the handful of peaceful repose.*

It's better to have a handful of quietness than both hands full and grasping for things you're not going to keep anyway. When you and I die, we're not going to take any of our possessions with us. When we die, we're not taking the corporation.

We've all heard the phrase "It's lonely at the top." Life doesn't have to be lonely at the top when we invite God into our relationships and stay humble enough to relate to others.

It's better to have a handful of quietness than to be a lonely worker. Through Solomon, God says you can choose to work less but have peace. Do you need help cutting back your work hours? Ask God to help you work faster. God can do more in five minutes than you and I can do in fifty-nine years. He's transformed situations for me when I've simply said, "God, I trust you. I can't get it done on my own, but You can show me how." He's an awesome help.

I tend to fall into the overworking, high achiever

trap. I'll never forget something my mother said to me one time because it's been very powerful in my life.

She said, "Marilyn, you are *driven* rather than *directed* by the Holy Spirit."

That was true, and God has had to deal with me about it over the years. If you're prone to this problem, please stop. Sit down. Choose to be God-sufficient, rather than self-sufficient. You'll enjoy life so much more. Remember, that's why Solomon wrote Ecclesiastes—to show you how to enjoy life!

Just as a person is a fool to be overly driven, a person is a fool to be lazy. Ask God for wisdom to acquire His intended handful for your life. Its reward is a more tranquil existence on this earth.

God instilled in us a desire for relationships. Clawing our way to the top of the corporate ladder, even to the point of knocking off our coworkers and stomping on them, isn't going to enhance our relationships or our enjoyment of life. Neither is ignoring our families, thinking we have to be the big provider or the best in our field.

Enjoyable life is found in giving, not in grasping for more. When you grasp, you're choosing life under the sun. Sooner or later, you're going to feel empty and shallow.

Believe me, you won't even enjoy your morning coffee. God didn't make us to live like that. If you'll choose the life of faith-filled giving under the Son over the life of taking, pessimism, and negativity under the sun, you can enjoy your family, friends, and coworkers. God made you to enjoy companionship, with Him and with others.

Many years ago I said, "Lord, I'm lonely. I don't have any friends. I see women going out to lunch and shopping together. But I can't do that. I can't live a normal life because I have all these Bible studies to teach and I'm a pastor's wife. I can't get too close to the people." I was whining about life under the sun.

The Lord said to me, "Have you ever asked Me for friends?"

"Well, no, not really."

"You always pick them out. Why don't you let Me give you friends?"

Folks, from that time forward, I have been so blessed with wonderful friends.

At times, I have traveled to other countries alone. But I didn't feel lonely. I could feel the beautiful presence of God and know He was traveling with me. I have found it isn't how many people you have around you, it's the One who lives inside you that satisfies.

I can be in an airport in a strange country all by myself, with no staff accompanying me, and be as happy as a lark because I have Him inside. Although my enjoyment of God on trips didn't happen overnight—I had to learn how to live life under the Son in those times rather than life under the sun—those trips alone have been some of my most precious times with God.

I especially love the next verses Solomon wrote. I hope you enjoy them as much as I do:

It's better to have a partner than go it alone.
Share the work, share the wealth.

And if one falls down, the other helps,
But if there's no one to help, tough!

Two in a bed warm each other.
Alone, you shiver all night.

By yourself you're unprotected.
With a friend you can face the worst.
Can you round up a third?
A three-stranded rope isn't easily snapped.

—*Ecclesiastes 4:9–12*

God made us to want a mate. I'm not saying every-body's going to get married, but we all need companion-ship. These verses tell us that's a good thing. When two people work together and stay focused going in the same direction, they receive a double reward.

Do you ever think you married the wrong person because your personalities are so opposite? Don't believe that lie! My husband and I are very different in our personalities. My daughter says we are extreme opposites. He's creative, laid back. I'm driven, focused!

You know, it's so good. Sometimes when I come home, weary and discouraged, I'll say to Wally, "I just don't think such and such will ever happen." But he'll say, "Marilyn, it will happen. It will."

Years ago when I was beginning to minister a little, we held a big conference where we invited a celebrity singer and some female models. We were fishing for lost people.

Everything went wrong. If I had planned it to go wrong, I couldn't have planned it any better. It was bad news!

I remember coming home and cooking.

My husband entered the kitchen and asked, "How are you?"

I whined, "I'm terrible. I'd like to run away and change my name."

The next day when I was cooking, he entered the kitchen again, but this time he held a beautifully wrapped gift.

Surprised, I asked, "What's this for?"

He explained, "It's for your birthday."

"Why," I said, "This is May! You know my birthday's in July."

With a twinkle in his eye, he said, "I know, but I thought if you're going to run away, you better have your gift early!"

When I was down, he lifted me up.

Many years ago, my husband went through a very dry time spiritually. He was a pastor, but he wasn't reading his Bible or praying. Living through that season felt awful.

But the Lord turned this time into something beautiful. He dealt with me: "Don't condemn him. Don't be on his case saying, 'Where's your Bible? Why aren't you in prayer meeting?' Instead, trust Me. Love him. Encourage him. Pray for him." I obeyed the Lord, and I fasted, too.

Out of the blue, one of my husband's friends came and ministered to him. As a result, I'm happy to say my husband has never gone through a spiritually dry time like that one again.

You see, we can warm our mates spiritually, as well as physically. And godly friendships are so important!

What if the devil assaults your mate? "By yourself you're unprotected. With a friend you can face the worst" (Eccles. 4:12). You're not going to lie down and play dead! This is how marriage can be powerful. When two stand together against something, their strength is doubled. That's why parents should back each other on discipline decisions.

The last half of 4:12 says, "A three-stranded rope isn't easily snapped." When you braid something, you take three strands and twist them together in a tight, strong arrangement. We can braid our marriages together with God in the center. No matter how different the personalities of a husband and wife, or how intense some of their seasons together, their three-stranded rope will not be easily broken.

I've been married more than fifty years. Let me tell you, my husband and I have had our times of fighting and disagreements. What has held us together? The three-stranded rope.

Do you want to enjoy your marriage? Bring God into it.

Companionship in marriage is a wonderful thing, but isolation due to self-sufficiency is not. To drive this point home, Solomon contrasts a poor but wise young man to an old and foolish king:

> A poor youngster with some wisdom is better off than an old but foolish king who doesn't know which end is up. I saw a youth just like this start with nothing and go from rags to riches, and I saw everyone rally to the rule of this young successor to the king.
>
> —*Ecclesiastes 4:13–15*

This king had once listened to advice, but isolated himself from his friends and advisers when he grew to think he was wiser than anyone else. When the king's young successor took the throne, this proud king who had no friends was forgotten by everyone.

I had the privilege of meeting the king of Jordan, King Abdullah II. I didn't approach him by saying, "Hi! I'm Marilyn Hickey and it sure is nice to meet you today!" Everyone knows not to address a king that way. No, I prepared myself to meet him in an honorable manner. I made sure I was dressed well, smelled fragrant, my hair was clean and styled, and my nails were painted.

When I was ushered in to meet the king, I was gracious and warm. I presented him with a gift I thought he'd enjoy.

However, I had heard the king was going to meet Bill Gates directly after meeting me. I figured Bill Gates would give the king a sizable financial gift, so I wondered what more I could give him. Then it occurred to me—I could give him prayer.

So when I met him, I said, "Your Majesty, I love to visit Muslim nations like yours and pray for the sick. Do you know what I would like? I would like the first names of your loved ones who are sick and the name of their illness, so I can personally pray for them."

The king was pleased.

I didn't meet King Abdullah II in a flippant manner, so why would I approach God in a disrespectful way? When we come into God's presence, we don't just say, "Hey, God! Hey, man upstairs!" No, we come with an attitude that He is a holy God. We honor Him.

Watch your step when you enter God's house.
Enter to learn. That's far better than mindlessly
    offering a sacrifice,
Doing more harm than good.

Don't shoot off your mouth, or speak before you
    think.
Don't be too quick to tell God what you think he
    wants to hear.
God's in charge, not you—the less you speak, the
    better.

Over-work makes for restless sleep.
Over-talk shows you up as a fool.

But against all illusion and fantasy and empty talk
There's always this rock foundation: Fear God!

—Ecclesiastes 5:1–3, 7

"Fear God" means "honor God." I want to communicate with Him, but to experience it, I must come ready to listen and obey, making sure I don't promise Him something I won't fulfill. We can't even begin to have a great relationship with the living God until we reverence and fear Him.

Part of a respectful relationship with God is honoring what He says to us and not adding anything to it. In other words, sometimes people have illusions that God said something He really didn't say. Sometimes they say God gave them a dream, when in reality, the dream stemmed from overwork or eating too much pizza late at night.

Your relationship with God is the most important relationship of all and is the source of your relationships with others. You will find Him to be the best companion you can ever have!

Do you work? Bring Him into your work relationships. Do you have a family? Ask God for help in your relationships with your children. Are you married? Ask God into that relationship. Are you in a leadership position? Don't live in that leadership position under the sun, merely accepting life as it is.

Why live frustrated with our relationships? Instead, we can look up, asking God for His supernatural wisdom to relate well with people in all kinds of situations and circumstances. God loves to answer simple, specific prayers, even in some bad circumstances.

One of my friends raised a daughter who was born again, Spirit-filled, and loved God. At work, she met a man and fell in love. They married, but he began to abuse her. They had a child together but their relationship continued to slide downhill.

Eventually, he left her. She changed jobs where she met a woman who was gracious and kind. Sadly, the woman was a lesbian and after a while, the two women started a relationship together. The child was living with them.

My friend lamented, "Marilyn, this is so discouraging to me."

I responded, "Well, let's believe God that this is going to change. Let's specifically say these words in prayer to the Lord: 'She is going to call and say, "Mom, I'm tired of this lifestyle. I want to come home." ' "

Every now and then, I would see my friend or she would call me. I would ask, "Well, did you hear from your daughter? Did she say, 'Mom, I'm tired of this lifestyle. I want to come home'?"

"No," she would say, "I haven't yet, but I'm going to!"

Five years went by. One day when I was in Pakistan, I received a wonderful e-mail. It read: "My daughter called me today and said, 'Mom, I'm tired of this lifestyle. I want to come home.' "

I'm telling you, you never know what God can do! We can make the mistake of getting hung up looking at things as they are right now instead of hung up looking at who He is. He is bigger than it all and He can do anything.

Where are you living today? "Don't fret or worry. Instead of worrying, pray. Let petitions and praises shape your worries into prayers, letting God know your concerns" (Phil. 4:6).

Specifically ask and simply trust. He makes everything beautiful in its time.

chapter 5

will i ever be content?

"The fear of the Lord is the beginning of wisdom" (Prov. 9:10 KJV). The most well-known wisdom book in the Bible is the book of Proverbs. I love it so much, I memorized the whole book one time! But I've grown to love Ecclesiastes, which is a wisdom book of the Bible along with Psalms, Proverbs, Song of Solomon, and Job.

Ecclesiastes is so full of practical, godly wisdom for our lives!

I want God's marks of wisdom in every area of my life. How about you?

Solomon continues his disclosure of life by talking to us about a wise financial lifestyle:

The one who loves money is never satisfied with money,

Nor the one who loves wealth with big profits.
More smoke.

—*Ecclesiastes 5:10*

If we choose to live an "I love money" under-the-sun lifestyle, even when our finances increase, our happiness won't. Life will still feel empty.

Some years ago, we knew a couple in our church who had been wonderfully born again. Prior to their salvation, the husband's alcoholism had shattered their marriage.

After they were born again, they asked God to fill them with His Holy Spirit. They were so thrilled with Jesus, they were in every church service, attending cell groups, reading their Bibles, and going all out for God.

The doctors said she would never bear children, but she became pregnant—with twins! Her husband was offered a job in another city and I hate to tell you this, but the job offer was in the pornography industry.

He approached Wally and me as he was trying to decide whether to take the job.

"What do you think?" he asked.

We said, "There's no thinking to it. Don't take it."

"But it's *double* my salary here," he moaned.

We said, "If it's triple, even if it's quadruple, no! *No!*"

He accepted the job and moved his family to another city where his wife gave birth to twins. Tragically, he started drinking again and divorced her.

He made more money, but it didn't satisfy. He ended up without a close companion to share it with.

When the enemy of your soul attacks, he's going to test your consecration to God. Do you love God for what you can get from Him or do you love Him? It's so much better to be content with what you have while believing God will meet your needs than to be greedily grasping for more.

We all know that financial problems tackle poor people, but do we ever stop and think about the financial challenges confronting rich people? Prosperity introduces problems no one ever wants to talk about, but Solomon does:

> When goods increase,
> They increase who eat them;
> So what profit have the owners
> Except to see them with their eyes?
>
> —*Ecclesiastes 5:11* NKJV

The more money you make, the more money you spend—on taxes, on maintenance, on employees, and family members. Just because it's coming in doesn't mean it's staying in. The money comes in, and the money goes out. You might as well wave good-bye to it.

Then Solomon reveals that the pressures of prosperity can render restless nights without sleep:

> The sleep of a laboring man *is* sweet,
> Whether he eats little or much;
> But the abundance of the rich will not permit him
> to sleep.
>
> —*Ecclesiastes 5:12* NKJV

Compared to the laboring man who is significantly poorer, the rich man is so busy taking care of his business transactions and investments that it's difficult for him to unwind at night. When he finally falls asleep, his mind may not rest as it wrestles with weighty decisions. Sleep is fitful because the rich man is worrying about financial matters.

Solomon addresses more drawbacks to prosperity:

> Here's a piece of bad luck I've seen happen:
> A man hoards far more wealth than is good for him
> And then loses it all in a bad business deal.
> He fathered a child but hasn't a cent left to give
> him.

He arrived naked from the womb of his mother;
He'll leave in the same condition—with nothing.
                              —Ecclesiastes 5:13–15

More money produces more financial capacity to yield to temptation. As Solomon discovered, people who choose a pleasure-indulging lifestyle over a godly, productive one have selected the unhappy and often dangerous life under the sun. To quote Solomon, pursuing pleasure is "Insane, Inane!" (Eccles. 2:2).

Many rich people have worked very hard to amass a fortune only to lose it. Some people lose it all, leaving nothing to their children. In some cases, they hired their lazy son who took over the family business and blew all the money. That's a problem!

Everyone enters the world with nothing and exits the same way. Eventually, rich people will forfeit all of their wealth because they can't take it with them when they die.

All his days he also eats in darkness,
And *he has* much sorrow and sickness and anger.

                              —*Ecclesiastes 5:17* NKJV

Another potentially dangerous problem for rich people is sickness caused from worrying about their money. "How can I hold on to it?" "How can I make more?"

"Who is trying to steal from me?" "Is my family safe?" Ulcers and other physical problems induced from anger and frustration over money challenges can make mealtime miserable.

Solomon clearly describes how prosperity can be a curse in our lives. Because of wealth, we can become ill or depressed, as well as endure the hatred of jealous people.

What is the remedy? Is it possible to be rich *and* content?

> Here is what I have seen: It is good and fitting for one to eat and drink, and to enjoy the good of all his labor in which he toils under the sun all the days of his life which God gives him; for it is his heritage. As for every man to whom God has given riches and wealth, and given him power to eat of it, to receive his heritage and rejoice in his labor—this is the gift of God.
>
> —*Ecclesiastes 5:18–19* NKJV

Solomon's verdict? Yes!

Does he say God wants you to enjoy life? Yes! Does he say God wants you to enjoy food? Yes! Does he say God wants you to enjoy beverages? Yes! Does he say God wants you to overeat and get drunk? Of course not!

Does he say when you work hard you should enjoy what you accomplished? Yes!

The alternative to the poverty- or prosperity-induced "I'm worried about money" lifestyle is the life under-the-Son lifestyle. How do you get it?

Ask God to transform your attitude about money. That way, wealth won't control you; living in God's financial wisdom, you'll be able to enjoy it. Money used God's way will bless you and others you know.

Ask Him for the power to enjoy your sleep, your food, and your health. Enjoying His gifts is living life under the Son instead of life under the sun. The ability to enjoy them is a *gift*, from God to you.

But that's not all God wants to give you:

> For he will not dwell unduly on the days of his
> life, because God keeps him busy with the joy of
> his heart.

> —*Ecclesiastes 5:20 NKJV*

One way God answers your request to enjoy life is by giving you joy in your heart. This joy is so fulfilling, you don't waste your time on earth regretting the past, dreading the future, or bored in the present.

God can keep you busy with joy in unusual places.

One time when I was standing in a crowded Chinese

train station, the Lord hit me with so much joy I thought I would explode!

Chinese people like operatic music with high-pitched vocals. I had heard it in the underground church where I had been ministering. Now I heard it again, just as I was thinking about how I was probably the only Westerner in the station, my red hair and fair skin contrasting sharply with the darker skin tone and black hair of the Chinese.

When I heard the high singing, I felt myself suddenly caught up into the presence of God. I almost felt Chinese, instead of American. I felt like I had the joy of China inside me.

What was that? It wasn't as though I was thrilled over a shopping bargain on high-fashion Chinese clothing, which I enjoy. God was simply keeping me busy with joy in my heart.

Interestingly, I have been in China twenty-four times and that joy from the Lord continues to bubble up inside me.

It's so wonderful how God can keep you busy, just being joyful and happy. We don't have to be wretched and miserable. In addition, He gives us the gift throughout our days of enjoying our labor as well as what we eat and drink.

Let me tell you another occasion when the Lord kept

me busy with joy in an unusual place. Many years ago, I was in El Salvador. My companions and I were driving through the jungles to give food and clothing to people in some of the labor camps during the war between the Contras and the Sandinistas.

At a certain point in our journey, we saw people selling mangoes under a canopy of trees. It was so hot and humid, we shouted to our driver, "Stop! Stop! We want to eat a mango!"

When we peeled the mangoes and sank our teeth into the fruit, the juice gushed out all over our faces and hands. What happened next was astonishing; the joy of the Lord hit two of us, one young man and me. He began to dance in the Lord, and I began to rejoice in God. I thought, *God, what is this? What's in the mango?*

But it wasn't the mango; it was God keeping us busy with joy.

Did you know God can keep you busy with joy in the middle of unusual circumstances?

The night my father died of a heart attack, I was with my weeping mother at the hospital. Later that night, I finally drove home. Grieving, I put myself to bed.

Sometime during the night, I was awakened by a warm sensation. I opened my eyes, and there beside the dresser stood an angel. A wonderful warmth emanated from him. Surprised but peaceful, I drifted back to sleep, only to be awakened some time later in the night by the same occurrence.

I asked the Lord, "Why are You doing this? Why are You blessing me like this at the time of my father's death?"

This is what He said to me: "I am letting you enter into a little of the glory that your father is living in."

God's warmth, peace, and joy flooded my soul. Its effect was so encompassing, it carried me all the way through my father's funeral. Although I grieved for my mother at her funeral, I can honestly say I did not grieve for my father at his. I'll never forget it—the funeral was December 24. I can still see the preacher reading from Revelation 21:2: "And I John saw the holy city, new Jerusalem"(KJV). My father's name was John. The preacher continued, "John is walking on the streets of the new Jerusalem." As I listened, I visualized my father alive and well in heaven, and I savored a portion of the glory I knew he was enjoying. God kept me busy with joy.

Will God keep you busy with joy when you face seemingly insurmountable odds?

When I was in Pakistan, I met a wonderful Spirit-filled priest who informed me, "Eighty percent of Pakistan is illiterate."

"Oh," I said, "I can't believe that!" But it was true. So I asked him, "How do you teach your people the Bible?"

He replied, "I'm a singer and God gives me songs. Every Sunday morning when I get up to preach, I sing the scriptures. I teach the congregation, from the oldest adult to the youngest child, to sing the scriptures we are studying that day. They continue to sing them for seven days. Oh, my congregation knows the Bible very well because we sing it."

I thought, *Wow! What is going on here? God is keeping that congregation busy with joy.* They're joyful in the Lord, learning God's Word even though they face great adversity. That beautiful priest was willing to tackle his country's illiteracy problem with faith-filled action, living life under the Son instead of settling for the pessimistic "what's the use" life under the sun.

Folks, if we allow Him, many times God will keep us joyful in the most unusual circumstances and places, even in situations that look hopeless. It's a tremendous experience.

Who can figure out life? Don't try—you'll scramble your brain. But I like what God says through Solomon in this verse:

And who knows what's best for us as we live out our meager smoke-and-shadow lives? And who can tell any of us the next chapter of our lives?

—*Ecclesiastes 6:12*

No one knows what's going to happen next. People are clueless. But we know poverty and prosperity can destroy poor and rich alike. We understand we can ask Jesus to exchange money misery for His wisdom and the ability to enjoy what our money buys for ourselves and others.

We know we are going to live through seasons of love and hate, peace and war, birth and death. We can choose to ask God into every season and believe He will make them beautiful. We sense there's more to life than our immediate existence, and we know we can ask Jesus to come inside and give us eternal life.

What is your choice? How are you looking at life? Ask yourself:

Am I complaining about my circumstances or am I viewing them as God does, from a position up above them?

Am I seeing life as the TV news presents it or from a prayerful change-the-news perspective?

Am I entertaining my mind so much that I don't notice the good God is doing around me?

Am I thinking predominantly negative, pessimistic thoughts, or am I thinking faith-filled thoughts that trust God for His best in my life?

chapter 6

giants and crazy-faith friends

Do people who choose the under-the-Son life of faith live in a fantasy world? What happens when hard times hit—does their faith survive?

How you answer this question determines your destiny.

"If we endure hardship, we will reign with him" (2 Tim. 2:12 NLT). Conversely, if we don't endure, we will not rule with Him. God rewards us when we fight the good fight of faith. Know this: The life of faith will take you through adversities, but the life without faith will drop you like a rock when distressing times strike.

"Let us run with endurance the race that is set before us, looking unto Jesus, the author and finisher of *our* faith" (Heb. 12:1–2 NKJV). Giants of adversity attack us all. God wants us to know how to slay them so we can enjoy our lives.

As baby boomers begin to age, one of the biggest giants many face is known as "midlife crisis." This is a time when people find themselves halfway through the race of life and they're tired. They don't want to endure life as it's been—they experience a strong desire for change.

Sometimes I think when we hit midlife, we feel bad about ourselves. We notice the first signs that we're halfway to death—wrinkles on our faces, weight gain, fatigue. Our attitude can get a little jaded; we're exhausted and cynical, yet we think we've arrived in life—everyone should listen to us and show respect.

But at the same time, we feel we don't fit in with young people. We're not completely tuned in to their music, clothing, hair, food, or style. Sometimes we feel like they look down on us.

When we work out at the gym, it doesn't help that our exercise clothes expose all of our fat. When I go to the gym, I can be on the treadmill at level 3.1 with an incline of 4, while the young person beside me is exercising at a 4.1 with an incline of 11. It's easy to be embarrassed, assuming she thinks I'm slow.

But a lot of these negative assumptions are simply the devil's lies. Most young people admire your effort to work out. They hope to be able to exercise at a 3.1 when they get older. We should watch out for these lies and keep pressing on for God's prize at life's finish line.

Don't allow yourself to get bogged down with depression or boredom at the midpoint of life. Look for ways to help someone. When I was sick with parasites, I learned a lot about how selfish I was. I realized all I could think about was how sick I felt. Choosing to call and pray with people lifted me out of my self-pity.

One giant opposing all of us from time to time is sadness:

A good reputation is better than a fat bank account.
Your death date tells more than your birth date.

—*Ecclesiastes 7:1*

Nothing's sadder than the death of someone we loved. And none of us likes to think about the day we're going to die, although we know it's inevitable our bodies will pass away. It's comforting to know our good names can outlive our bodies, leaving behind a good aroma when people remember us.

Solomon compares bad times to good times, revealing how God views them both. Are you ready for this?

You learn more at a funeral than at a feast—
After all, that's where we'll end up. We might
discover something from it.

—*Ecclesiastes 7:2*

When we feel sadness and pressure, that's when we look to God, asking Him to teach us. We learn more when we fast than when we overfeed ourselves.

I was in a time of sadness during those seven months when I couldn't go to work, couldn't eat much, couldn't walk very far, and couldn't fly anywhere. Oh, it was a terrible time in my life! But I tell you, I will never forget those seven months because they were some of the most precious times I've ever had with God. He talked to me and taught me. I learned more when I couldn't accomplish anything than in many previous years of achievement and accomplishments.

One thing the Lord taught me was I needed to speak what He said rather than what I felt. That became a key concept for me.

Did you know giants have ears? When the shepherd boy David confronted the giant Goliath, the first thing he did was tell the giant he was going to kill him.

The Bible didn't tell us to talk *about* our mountains; it said to talk *to* our mountains (Mark 11:23). Did you know your mountains have ears? They're waiting to hear what you'll say.

One of my friends helped me speak God's truth about my situation. When you're going through a sad, pressure-filled season, it's tremendously important to have "crazy-faith friends." Like the paraplegic's friends in Mark 2:2–12 who cut a hole in the roof above Jesus' head and lowered their friend on a stretcher to His feet to be healed, these crazy-faith friends don't merely feel sorry for you. They are friends who boldly proclaim, "God can turn this around!" and then act to help you. Ask God for these friends—friends who are full of faith, who love you, and who will believe miracles are possible in your life.

Every day during my time of pressure and mourning, I called a crazy-faith friend and talked to her for five or ten minutes.

She would ask me, "Did you have a good day today?"

Sometimes I did and sometimes I didn't.

"Well, it was a little better than yesterday," I'd reply.

One day she said to me, "This is your last bad day. From now on, you are going to have good days." She reminded me of the date.

The next morning when I woke up, I called her.

She said, "Do you feel good?"

"No, not particularly," I confessed.

My body was still shaking inside. I still hadn't been able to sleep. But I wrote down "Yesterday was my last bad day. This is a good day."

Do you know what? My day was better. The next day I wrote down "This is a good day" and I kept writing it down every day for about three months. I added scriptures with faith confessions. For example, I wrote down "Casting all your care upon Him, for He cares for you" (1 Pet. 5:7 NKJV). Then I said the verse aloud, personalizing it: "Lord, I cast my worry on You, because I know You love me."

Another verse I wrote was "And He said to me, 'My grace is sufficient for you, for My strength is made perfect in weakness.' Therefore most gladly I will rather boast in my infirmities, that the power of Christ may rest upon me" (2 Cor. 12:9 NKJV). Then I said aloud: "Thank You that your grace is sufficient for me. Thank You that Your strength is made perfect in me. Thank You that the power of Christ rests on me."

Finally, I felt so good I had to write down something better! "I am better than before. I have more energy and more anointing than I did before," I noted.

When did I learn to speak what God says rather than how I feel? I learned it in the time of mourning. Please understand, I'm not inviting the devil to attack your life or mine. I'm simply saying if you choose to look above to Him, He will take your mourning time and teach you how to improve your life.

A second lesson God taught me during that time of sadness and mourning purified my motives.

Crying is better than laughing.
It blotches the face but it scours the heart.

Sages invest themselves in hurt and grieving.
Fools waste their lives in fun and games.

—*Ecclesiastes 7:3–4*

When troubles come, we have a choice. We can divert ourselves from the sadness and pain by watching eighty-nine movies, or we can look up to Him instead.

When I was in that time of severe sickness, God spoke to me about some things He wasn't pleased with in my life. The major thing He spoke to me about was pride.

He said, "You have pride in areas where you are self-sufficient instead of God-sufficient." Then He pinpointed those areas. Let me tell you, He didn't mince any words.

I informed my son-in-law, Reece. "God told me I have a lot of pride and these are the areas."

His reply was so sweet. "Oh," he said, "I don't think you have a lot of pride."

I admitted, "But God does." And I repented of it.

During my time of great sickness and sadness, I looked to God and He searched my heart. When I repented, my heart was cleansed. He made my heart better!

Every now and then, I can feel pride creeping back into my heart. I quickly repent to keep my heart pure before the Lord. God hates pride: "First pride, then the crash—the bigger the ego, the harder the fall" (Prov. 16:18).

Another giant Solomon identifies is a rebuke from a wise person.

You'll get more from the rebuke of a sage
Than from the song and dance of fools.

—*Ecclesiastes 7:5*

None of us likes to be reprimanded, but it's one way we learn. I've learned a great deal from rebukes—I don't like them, I don't want to hear them, but they're good for me. Some rebukes we receive aren't going to be right, because some people will put us down out of jealousy. But when two or three people tell you the same thing, watch out how you respond! You better check it out. How do you handle adversity? When hard times hit, do you choose life under the Son, leaning on the Lord?

Solomon addresses what adversity can do if we choose life under the sun. He warns against the dangerous responses of compromise, anger, and ungratefulness.

Surely oppression destroys a wise *man's* reason,
And a bribe debases the heart.

—*Ecclesiastes 7:7* NKJV

Adversity can make you feel like you're losing your mind. You can get to the point where you exclaim, "What's the use! Why serve God? I can't handle the pressure."

Sometimes when people experience financial adversity, they get into some sticky things, like the man who accepted the job in the pornographic industry and then lost his health and family. Great giants of greed ganged up on him. He could have rejected the job and believed God for financial increase. Instead, he accepted the bribe, compromising his faith.

Too bad he didn't choose God's way out—trusting and obeying Him. Don't yield to temptation. Slay your giants or they will slay you.

When you're going through a time of adversity where a giant is staring you down, remember this:

Endings are better than beginnings.

—*Ecclesiastes 7:8*

YOUR GIANT IS TEMPORARY.

There is an end to every trial. When I was so sick, some days I would say to myself ten times a day, "This is temporary. I'm not going to feel this way forever. The end is going to be better than the beginning." I had to fight hard because my giant of adversity overshadowed every aspect of my life: I shook inside all the time, my stomach burned constantly, I couldn't eat, the smell of food nauseated me, the doctors couldn't find out what was wrong with me, and even though I am not a depressed person, I was extremely depressed from this giant clubbing me physically, emotionally, and mentally. The devil battered me with thoughts such as, *This is the end of you. You will never board a plane again. You will never preach again.*

At my lowest point, I had a thought to drive up into the mountains, pick one out, and drive off it. Even though I was too sick to drive, I managed to shakily crawl inside my car. Clinging to the wheel, I drove up several mountains in the area where we live, finding one I could probably drive off.

But then a voice spoke inside my heart: *This isn't godly wisdom. This is temporary. You are looking at what is the seen circumstance, but it is temporary.*

That voice was so strong, I turned around and drove home.

Your circumstance is temporary. What you're going through will not last forever.

Here I am today, flying in airplanes, speaking in countries all over the world, and with more energy than I enjoyed in my thirties.

A missionary from Spain ministered to me, saying, "Marilyn, the end is going to be better than the beginning. When you come out of this, you are going to have more open doors, you are going to do more things for God, and you are going to see some unusual things happen to you." I'm delighted to report this has all come true.

Don't let these times of adversity kill you. Choose life under the Son and kill your giant. Grab a hold of the hope that your trials will end.

Solomon's next warning is powerful:

Don't be quick to fly off the handle.
Anger boomerangs. You can spot a fool by the
    lumps on his head.

—*Ecclesiastes 7:9*

Solomon's warning? Don't tolerate anger and frustration so long they become a permanent part of your personality. There are a lot of angry people walking around. It's so much better to be honest with God, asking and trusting Him for help with specific needs.

I know we want our adverse circumstances to change in twenty-four seconds, twenty-four hours, or twenty-four days. But we have to choose to be patient, and while we're waiting and waiting and waiting, we have to remember our situation is temporary—the end is coming!

When I lost so much weight I looked like skin and bones, I would walk into our church and people would greet me so sweetly. They'd smile and say, "You look so good! You know, every day you're getting better!" Well, I knew I looked awful!

I asked our church to pray I would gain weight. I remember the moment I stood on the scale and discovered I had gained one pound! I kept gaining weight to the point where I had to ask them to quit praying!

It wasn't easy waiting for my health to improve. But

God says waiting is good for us. He will give us His life under the Son when we stay patient and watch for His supernatural touch to change our circumstances.

Finally, Solomon warns against a discontented, ungrateful attitude:

> Don't always be asking, "Where are the good old
>   days?"
> Wise folks don't ask questions like that.
>
> —*Ecclesiastes 7:10*

We tend to think life was better "way back when" in a simpler era. But everyone throughout history has faced giants of adversity. We can't focus on Jesus while looking at the past.

Time stress is one of the biggest giants people face today. Trying to juggle it all—spouse, kids, sports and music activities, work, exercise, Bible study, prayer, friends, the never ending to-do list—tempts us to yearn for the good old days. "There's not enough time to get it all done!" is a familiar lament.

So how can we combat this everyday adversary?

I can tell you what helps me. I begin my day in bed declaring my thanks to God for the gift of a new day! When I get up, I fix a cup of coffee. As I enjoy it, I pull out my personal list of scriptures to read and speak over my day. Remember the scriptures I wrote down and confessed when I was ill? I continue to speak them to this day.

One meaningful scripture I say is "I am crucified with Christ: nevertheless I live; yet not I, but Christ liveth in me: and the life which I now live in the flesh I live by the faith of the Son of God, who loved me, and gave himself for me" (Gal. 2:20 KJV). I personalize it by saying, "I am dead to sin. I live by faith in the Son."

Reading and personalizing several scriptures aloud between sips of coffee helps settle me as I head into my day. I'm enabled to see the circumstances I'm facing that day from God's viewpoint rather than from my human under-the-sun viewpoint. I can't express how important confessing scriptures is except to reiterate that helping us see our lives from an under-the-Son perspective is why Solomon wrote the wonderful wisdom book of Ecclesiastes.

After I confess my list of scriptures, I write down ten things Jesus is to me for that particular day. For example, "Jesus is my peace today" and "The Holy Spirit is my helper." Then I tear them up and throw them away, knowing I will repeat this exercise the next day.

Thanking the Lord and personalizing scriptures start my day well, directed by the power of the Holy Spirit.

The second thing I do you may not like.

I exercise for an hour. Isn't that disgusting? But I've found exercise enhances my mind, my emotions, and my body. By nature, I'm not a physically active person. I never liked sports in high school, and even now I don't like to watch football. I'll watch basketball because it's a fast-paced sport.

To me, the best thing about exercise is after a while, it's over! But I have to admit exercise helps me think clearer, feel happier, and enjoy physical stamina. I've become a big exercise fan because I want to feel well the next ten years of my life as I embark on overseas crusades.

How do you want to feel the next ten years of your life? Do you want to enjoy them?

It's easy to become angry and impatient when we face obstacles. It's easy to yield to temptation and consider taking a bribe. It's easy to feel like you're losing your mind when you're intimidated by a giant. It's easy to feel like quitting and retreating to an easier past.

But we can slay our giants by believing God will take our situation and do something good in the middle of it. We can speak the Word of God to our giants.

Yes, faith does survive troublesome times. What's more, Solomon discovered another key to living an enjoyable life in the middle of hard times. Let's take a look.

chapter 7

wisdom to enjoy life

What's going to breathe life into your soul when adversity threatens to destroy you? God's wisdom!

> Wisdom is better when it's paired with money,
> Especially if you get both while you're still living.
> Double protection: wisdom and wealth!
> Plus this bonus: Wisdom energizes its owner.

> —*Ecclesiastes 7:11–12*

When I was ill, the doctors asked me to check into the hospital to run some tests. The first morning there, I saw what appeared to be a black cloud coming in through the window. It moved over to my bed where I sensed it hovering over me. Frightened and depressed, I asked the Lord, "What is this?" I needed God's wisdom to deliver me.

He reminded me of something that happened to me when I was eleven years old. It happened during World War II when my parents brought our family to live with an aunt and uncle. During that time, my uncle sexually abused me. Overcome with guilt, I didn't tell my parents. Somehow, I thought it was my fault.

Later, in prayer with two friends, God revealed to me how a terrible, dark fear entered me back then—so terrible, I tried to commit suicide. The fear had magnified inside my mind from thinking I was totally alone. I thought God had abandoned me.

"You thought I had abandoned you, but I was there all the time," He said to me. He showed me how He brought me out of that situation. My father found a place for us to live so we were able to leave my uncle's house. I was able to attend a junior high school, become a valedictorian, and then best of all, I became born again. God had been with me all along, leading me out of danger.

I was amazed to learn this. Now that I was able to look back over my life and see how God had been working behind the scenes to deliver me, I realized I hadn't been alone after all.

The dark cloud of fear lifted and I was able to experience a normal pattern of sleep. God's wisdom for my situation revived my soul.

God is there with you all the time. He will give you a special wisdom that perfectly fits your circumstance to take you through. Ask Him for it: "If you don't know what you're doing, pray to the Father. He loves to help. You'll get his help, and won't be condescended to when you ask for it" (James 1:5). When a giant looms over you, God's wisdom will dispel its shadow.

What more does Solomon reveal about life?

In the day of prosperity be joyful,
But in the day of adversity consider:
Surely God has appointed the one as well as the
    other . . .

—*Ecclesiastes 7:14* NKJV

We feel really good when we're prospering, don't we? It's wonderful when everything is going well.

But in the day of adversity, don't have a nervous breakdown! Don't backslide. Think about what's happening; learn from it because God has designated both kinds of days to keep us looking to Him.

When you prosper, you could backslide, quit reading your Bible, quit going to church, quit serving God, leave your wife or husband, and abandon your children. Prosperity is not your key to enjoying life.

Neither is adversity. Some people, even born-again Christians, who suffer adversity lose their minds. Christians facing adversity can yield to temptation.

But God wants to bring you through prosperity and adversity victoriously. Keep looking up, believing God is working on your behalf—catch Him doing something good for you!

No one has discovered the key to understanding everything that happens in life. There isn't one. We tend to ask, "Why does this happen?" or "Why did I lose this loved one at such a young age?" We are never going to understand it all.

So then, what can we do? We can look for wisdom. Why?

Wisdom puts more strength in one wise person
Than ten strong men give to a city.

—*Ecclesiastes 7:19*

God's wisdom will strengthen you when your body is weak. Wisdom will strengthen you when your mind and emotions are collapsing. Wisdom will strengthen you when your family turns against you. Wisdom will strengthen you when the devil is breathing down your neck. Wisdom will strengthen you to come through whatever you're going through.

What weapon can you wield to kill the giant? The wisdom of God.

When you're weak, God is strong on your behalf. "Finally . . . be strong in the Lord and in the power of His might" (Eph. 6:10 NKJV).

The young shepherd boy David killed the giant Goliath through the wisdom of God. He didn't have a sword. He didn't have any armor. When King Saul tried to give him armor, David wouldn't wear it. He wanted to defeat the giant God's way.

Through the wisdom of God, David declared to the giant, "This day the LORD will deliver you into my hand, and I will strike you and take your head from you" (1 Sam. 17:46 NKJV). David ran to meet Goliath, reached in his bag, removed a stone, and slung it from his slingshot. The stone sank in the giant's forehead, felling him facedown to the ground. David dashed over and removed the giant's own sword from its sheath to cut off the behemoth's head.

The wisdom of God delivered David from his giant!

Prosperity can destroy you, and adversity can destroy you, but the wisdom of God can bring you through victoriously.

Let's discover something else God's wisdom will do:

A man's wisdom makes his face shine,
And the sternness of his face is changed.

—*Ecclesiastes 8:1* NKJV

You can face so much stress your face droops to the floor, but the moment you get a word from the Lord, your face begins to shine. Suddenly, you find yourself smiling although your circumstances haven't changed a bit.

But you've changed—on the inside and the outside. And when you win the battle on the inside, you're going to win it on the outside.

When King Solomon asked God for wisdom to govern Israel, God blessed him with three kinds of wisdom. One of those was Sophia wisdom. "Sophia," is a Greek word meaning "the wisdom of ultimate things."

Sophia is a girl's name. Throughout the wisdom book of Proverbs, you'll notice that wisdom is always referred to as a woman who brings you joy and victory. When I noticed this I joked, *Is that because women are smarter than men?* Oh no, that's not it!

A woman is the one who submits; she is the submissive partner in a marriage relationship. Here's the point: To get the wisdom of God, you have to submit to Him, choosing life under the Son. God's Sophia wisdom is available to every believer in his time of prosperity and his time of adversity. You don't have to be killed by prosperity giants, and you don't have to be killed by adversity giants. The wisdom of God as you live submitted to the Son will take you through victoriously.

One of the reasons I love Ecclesiastes is because a man who esteemed wisdom wrote it.

When he first became king, God appeared to Solomon in a dream one night and asked him, "What do you want?" Solomon answered, "I want wisdom." God was very pleased he asked for this, just as He is pleased when you and I ask for wisdom. God gave Solomon more wisdom than anyone had ever had before, plus two things he didn't ask for: more riches and honor than any other king during his lifetime (see 1 Kings 3:5–13).

Solomon didn't want wisdom so he could show it off like a smart aleck; he wanted understanding to govern Israel wisely. He ruled in godly wisdom for a while.

One of the most famous stories showcasing the wisdom God gave Solomon occurred the day two arguing women approached the king. They were fighting over a little boy, both claiming to be his mother. Godly wisdom prompted Solomon to command, "Bring me a sword! Divide the living child in two, and give half to one, and half to the other." Immediately, the true mother of the child exclaimed, "Oh my lord, give her the living child, and by no means kill him!" Solomon promptly returned the child to the woman who saved the child's life, because it was obvious she was the true mother (1 Kings 3:16–27 NKJV).

Do you need wisdom? Life is more enjoyable when God's wisdom helps us conquer our giants. God loves you and is faithful to give you wisdom when you ask for it.

I believe when you give to others, God has more opportunity to give you wisdom to defeat your problems. If you're facing adversity, think of people who are troubled by sickness, poverty, a painful relationship, or a harmful habit. Believe God will touch them and turn their situation around.

chapter 8

life is fragile: enjoy it!

Life is fragile. We don't know if we have tomorrow.

Before the tsunami hit, did its victims know it was coming? Did they think, *Tomorrow I won't be here. In ten minutes everything will be destroyed?*

We don't know which day will be our last. Every day is a gift God wants us to enjoy.

Throughout the Bible, God continually emphasizes today living. A few instances are "Give us this day our daily bread" (Matt. 6:11 KJV), "This is the day the Lord has made" (Ps. 118:24 NKJV), and ". . . do not worry about tomorrow" (Matt. 6:34 NKJV).

It's wise to esteem today, knowing life on earth doesn't last forever.

In his pursuit for life's meaning, Solomon learned some things to help us enjoy living.

One thing he found out was if we submit to author-ity instead of always challenging it, our lives will be more enjoyable. Why? Because authority can keep you from harm. You'll live a safer life.

> Where the word of a king *is, there is* power;
> And who may say to him, "What are you doing?"
> He who keeps his command will experience
>   nothing harmful;
> And a wise man's heart discerns both time and
>   judgment,
> Because for every matter there is a time and
>   judgment,
> Though the misery of man increases greatly.
>
> —*Ecclesiastes 8:4–6* NKJV

Solomon says a wise man recognizes authority and the judgment that comes if he doesn't yield to it. A stupid man doesn't recognize authority or the consequences that come from failing to submit to it. Worse yet, his life becomes even more miserable.

We have to come under authority if we want God to move in a situation or circumstance. We see horrible things about teenagers hurting their parents on the news. In most cases, these teenagers probably haven't been taught biblical principles and values. For instance, "Honor your father and mother" is the first commandment that has a promise attached to it, namely, "so you will live well and have a long life" (Eph. 6:2–3). You know, we're not even supposed to display the Ten Commandments in some public places anymore, so authority principles aren't as prevalent in society as they once were.

Authority principles start in the home with parents. "And you, fathers, do not provoke your children to wrath, but bring them up in the training and admonition of the Lord" (Eph. 6:4 NKJV).

Children don't train parents; parents train them. Children don't admonish parents; parents admonish them. When children submit to their parents, life will go well for them and they can live a long life.

When children leave home to attend school, teachers have authority over them. In society, police have authority. In church, pastors have authority.

Traveling to many countries exposes me to many lifestyles. Overseas, it's not uncommon for parents to select the mate for their child. Youths in America would have a nervous breakdown if parents even suggested it. In India, Christian parents choose the husband or wife for their child. In Pakistan, the same is not uncommon. It's also not uncommon in Syria among Armenian believers.

Most of these marriages are happy. Much less divorce occurs in these countries. Why? Because they believe their parents love them enough to make the right choice, and they believe God can give them love for their mates.

Now I know I'm rattling your cage, but it's good for you.

What does Solomon say? God has a time and a judgment. It may not come right away, but it's going to come. So submit to authority. You don't want to be under the judgment; you want to be under the blessing.

Now, there are some things no one has authority over:

No one has power over the spirit to retain the spirit,
And no one has power in the day of death.
There is no release from that war,
And wickedness will not deliver those who are
    given to it.

—*Ecclesiastes 8:8* NKJV

When it's time for you to go home, your spirit is going to go. The Bible also speaks of certain end-time wars and the Antichrist who will rise to power. We wish we had authority over these occurrences, but we don't. In the end, the sinfulness of wicked rulers will destroy them.

Another thing Solomon learned was to keep fearing God even in the face of injustice.

All this I observed as I tried my best to under-stand all that's going on in this world. As long as men and women have the power to hurt each other, this is the way it is.

Because the sentence against evil deeds is so long in coming, people in general think they can get by with murder.

Even though a person sins and gets by with it hundreds of times throughout a long life, I'm still convinced that the good life is reserved for the person who fears God, who lives reverently in his presence.

—Ecclesiastes 8:9,11–12

Though you don't see people getting caught right away, Solomon advises against losing your fear of God. Because the fear of God is the beginning of wisdom, if you lose your fear of Him, I'm telling you, you'll lose His wisdom. It's easy to say, "Look how long it's taking for justice to be served," and begin to lose your fear of God. Remember this: Someday, justice will be served. Place the timing in God's hands.

Do you know it's good for you to get caught early? If people don't get caught when they begin to do something wrong, they'll keep doing it on a larger scale. They'll become more evil.

It's the same way with our mouths: "Let no corrupt communication proceed out of your mouth" (Eph. 4:29 KJV) because corruption has a way of multiplying. Sin should be dealt with quickly before it grows.

I was caught cheating on a test in sixth grade. The teacher saw me looking over on another student's paper, then writing on my own, looking over again, then writing on my own over and over again. The teacher exposed me in front of the whole class. I was so embarrassed, I thought I would never be able to walk into that classroom again. But of course, I did.

I was a good student, and it was ridiculous I hadn't studied. It was good for me to get caught early before I made a habit of cheating.

How do you handle injustice?

Many years ago when Sarah was a baby, one of my neighbors was a woman whose husband had an affair and left her on her own to raise four young daughters.

I tried to help her by talking to her, praying with her, witnessing to her, and giving food and gifts to her. But all she could ever talk about was what her husband had done to her. She was so bitter! She was not a born-again Christian.

Sadly, she raised her four daughters in that bitterness. When I see her daughters today, they say the same things their mother said. They're stuck on how wrong their father was.

Well, they're right—he was wrong. He inflicted an injustice on them all. But bitterness can become a curse that is passed from generation to generation.

When injustice hits home, we have a choice: we can become hard, bitter, and vindictive, or we can keep our hearts soft and clean by praying and believing God to meet our specific needs.

Enjoying life under the Son is so much more enjoyable than worrying and complaining about injustices that are a part of life under the sun. If you decide to live a life of faith under authority, when injustice bites, God will work to turn your situation around.

Did you know you can change injustice through prayer? When I was sick in bed with parasites, I would turn on the TV and watch the news. Oh, a lot of that news was very depressing. But the Lord said to me, "You can pray over the news and change it." So I began to pray over the news and I saw answers to my prayers.

Don't stop believing when you don't see the answer to your prayer right away. When I prayed for the removal of Ceausescu, the corrupt leader of Romania, I thought God would remove such an evil man within thirty days, but He didn't. But within months, God answered my prayers.

Will you choose to give up or will you stay in faith? Live a life of faith.

You make the choice.

Don't forget—faith has a reward! "But without faith *it is* impossible to please *Him,* for he who comes to God must believe that He is, and *that* He is a rewarder of those who diligently seek Him" (Heb. 11:6 NKJV). He will work things out for you.

Solomon continues:

So, I'm all for just going ahead and having a good time—the best possible. The only earthly good men and women can look forward to is to eat and drink well and have a good time—compensation for the struggle for survival these few years God gives us on earth.

—*Ecclesiastes 8:15*

Eating and drinking encourage us in our daily lives as we live under authority and experience injustices. They provide enjoyable God-given breaks in each day.

Solomon writes to us in such practical terms! He tells us something important to keep in mind.

Go, eat your bread with joy,
And drink your wine with a merry heart;

For God has already accepted your works.
Let your garments always be white,
And let your head lack no oil.

—*Ecclesiastes 9:7–8* NKJV

In Solomon's time, oil was a symbol for joy. Do you know if you eat with depression you can make yourself sick but if you eat with joy you get more out of your food? Medical experts have proven that.

What else is Solomon saying? We can choose to be pessimistic; we can choose to be negative when we witness injustices. Or we can choose to believe God will bring a victory.

I took another walk around the neighborhood and
    realized that on this earth as it is—
The race is not always to the swift,
Nor the battle to the strong,
Nor satisfaction to the wise,
Nor riches to the smart,
Nor grace to the learned.
Sooner or later bad luck hits us all.

No one can predict misfortune.
Like fish caught in a cruel net or birds in a trap,

So men and women are caught
By accidents evil and sudden.

—*Ecclesiastes 9:11–12*

The fastest, the strongest, the world's wisest, the smartest, and the skilled are not guaranteed success. Time limitations and unexpected events occur in everyone's lives.

How can you live well in the time you have? How can you enjoy life despite all the negative circumstances it throws you? By keeping your faith in Him and letting Him teach you how to enjoy life, instead of whining and groaning about it and falling apart.

Life is delicate and unpredictable, but two things are sure:

1. The fear of God will stand.
2. Faith in God will stand.

That means, no matter what you're facing, if you will keep honoring and trusting God, you will come out all right.

Have you ever struggled so much with an adversary that you feel only a real-life hero or heroine could possibly win?

Would you like to be a hero? Written in the Greek

and Hebrew languages, the Bible includes four Hebrew words describing "man" in the Old Testament, with only one describing man as a "hero."

It isn't "adam," meaning "earthly or carnal" used in Ecclesiastes 1:3 NKJV: "What profit has a man from all his labor In which he toils under the sun?" nor is it "'iysh," referring to "reciprocal relationship" used in Ecclesiastes 9:15 NKJV: "Now there was found in it a poor wise man, and he by his wisdom delivered the city. Yet no one remembered that same poor man." It also isn't "'enowsh," meaning "weak, sickly, sinful" and used in Ecclesiastes 12:3 NKJV: "In the day when the keepers of the house tremble, And the strong men bow down."

But it is the word "geber," meaning "hero" used in Psalm 34:8 NKJV: "Oh, taste and see that the LORD is good; Blessed is the man who trusts in Him!"

Who is a hero to God? A person who trusts Him!

Do you trust God? If you do, you're a hero.

Did you notice only three Hebrew words for man were described in the book of Ecclesiastes? "Geber," the hero word for man, was left out. This ties back in with Solomon's purpose for writing Ecclesiastes. He wanted to illustrate the meaninglessness of life when we don't trust God, in an effort to point us toward becoming faith-filled heroes. Solomon appeals to the reasoning powers of pessimistic people, portraying how empty life feels when God isn't trusted.

He would know—sadly, for a period of time, Solomon rejected godly wisdom and worshipped the idols of his foreign wives. Without God, he despaired and focused on ungodly ways to achieve contentment.

Thankfully, he repented and returned to God for the source of his joy. Through Ecclesiastes, Solomon wanted to whet our appetite for God, our source of enjoyment of life. He wanted to convey that hope in our daily lives springs from trusting God, actively watching for Him to appear in the little things that happen to us during our waking hours. After he returned to the true Shepherd, he looked back on life and summed it up for you and me: Fear God and have fun!

Catching God doing something good on your behalf will plaster a smile all over your face. Your enthusiasm will be contagious to people around you, making them happier and making you a person of influence, partnering with God to brighten the lives of others.

chapter 9

enjoying life in uncertain times

Troubles and uncertainties are a part of life, but even in those times we can enjoy our lives through trusting in God and asking for His wisdom. Knowing He loves us helps us feel secure.

Some years ago when I was in Pakistan, I was invited to be a guest on a secular, call-in television program, similar to *Good Morning Pakistan*.

Uncertain about saying the wrong thing, I asked, "What do you want me to talk about?" I was very concerned about getting in trouble, consequently having my crusade cancelled and my visa revoked.

They responded, "The topic will be healing. People will call in with questions about it."

I agreed.

A woman called in and said, "You say that you pray

to God in the name of Jesus and He heals the sick but couldn't you pray to God in the name of Muhammed, or Confucius, or Buddha and get the same results?"

At that moment, I needed God's light to answer wisely. Job 29:3 describes how God counsels us: "I walked through the dark by [His] light."

As quickly as you can snap your fingers, He enlightened me. I heard myself say, "Well, you know, I don't have any experience praying in the name of Muhammed or Confucius or Buddha, so I can't tell you. But I have a lot of experience praying in the name of Jesus, and I've seen many healings and miracles."

And you know what? Nobody got upset. Nobody got mad. I've been allowed to visit Pakistan four times since that time when God's wisdom shone and took me through the darkness.

Does God always bring the wisdom you need that fast? No, sometimes it can come very fast, and sometimes it's a process. But He gives it when you need it. Don't give up trusting Him for it. Faith is a positive, powerful force.

God will shine a lamp into the darkness of your cynical, critical, ugly time where you're thinking, *What's the use?* He'll remind you, *Let me give you some light in your darkness. I have a purpose in this. I have a plan. I have a passion for you."*

But faith does nothing apart from God's Word. "So then faith comes by hearing, and hearing by the word of God" (Rom. 10:17 NKJV).

You can think positive thoughts all day, but folks, when you do that, you're merely living on the same realm as your problem. You need to find a higher realm that transcends the realm of your problem. Move on up to the heart of the matter—move up to the realm of faith. That's the realm of the power of the Holy Spirit.

In this wonderful book of Ecclesiastes, Solomon isn't afraid to expose the issues of the heart.

Did you know all of your issues originate in your heart?

It's common to hear people today saying, "Oh, she's like that because she has issues" or "He has an anger issue."

Is there help for people? God's Word and His Holy Spirit can change our hearts, improving what we do, say, and think.

We can choose God's ways or we can choose to be foolish. Foolishness is characterized by doing stupid things, living a surface-level and silly life. A foolish person isn't a thinker and chooses not to meditate on scriptures or choose a life of faith.

Solomon exposes the difference between foolishness and wisdom:

Dead flies in perfume make it stink, And a little foolishness decomposes much wisdom.

—*Ecclesiastes 10:1*

You can start out saying, "I'm going to walk with God. I'm going to walk in His anointing. I'm going to walk in His wisdom." But if you take a little detour and get off course, you can get in a lot of trouble. You may have smelled wonderful before, full of goodness, but then just a little bit of folly and foolishness made you stink, destroying the wisdom you had shown in the past.

Years ago, when I first started to teach the Bible, long before I was on radio or television, I would invite people from our church and other church denominations in our community to come on specific Friday nights to study a book of the Bible. Those were special occasions, and we had a great time together. People would invite Jesus into their lives. People would ask the Holy Spirit to fill them.

There was a man from our own church who would always attend. He would hang around afterward, wanting to talk to me. I felt uncomfortable about it.

He would say to me, "If you need a ride home, I'll take you home."

I would think, *If I do that, it will have an appearance of evil. The Bible says shun the appearance.* If you shun the appearance, you are not going to get into evil.

Therefore, I would always say, "No, I have my car. Everything's fine." But one night, I got in my car and it wouldn't start!

He was standing next to my car because his car was parked beside mine. He said, "Oh, don't worry. I'll take you home."

I said, "Well, I'll call my husband first because he might want to come and get me."

To my chagrin, Wally's response was, "Oh, let him take you home. No problem." But you know, inside I had a funny feeling.

On the way home, the man said, "You know, I am very attracted to you."

I almost fell out of the car! Now remember, just a little folly can affect the anointing and favor and wisdom that you've been living in. So I thought, *Oh, be careful.*

And you know, God gave me the light I needed for that occasion. I said, "No, you are not attracted to me. You have a gorgeous wife. She is much prettier than I am. What you are attracted to is the anointing of God when I teach the Word. You're thinking it's an attraction to me but you're attracted to the Word of God. I just love your wife and I'm going to call her tomorrow and tell her what you said to me tonight because we don't want you to get off track and I don't want to get off track."

He didn't know what to say.

When I got out of the car that night, I told my husband about it. He kind of laughed. And I did call the man's wife.

Do you know to this day, over thirty years later, we are still friends with that couple!

You may think, *Well, that was such a small thing.* But a little thing can make you stink and flush your wisdom down the drain.

Maybe you've gotten into a little folly, a little foolishness. Good news—you can decide to get out. You can make a choice from your heart to live in godly wisdom rather than the world's wisdom, which is foolishness. The world's way of living under the sun leads to bad results that you won't want to find yourself entangled in. Right choices bring right results.

Wise thinking leads to right living;
Stupid thinking leads to wrong living.

—*Ecclesiastes 10:2*

Now that man from my story was into some stupid thinking. But you know, he turned around! From that moment, he has lived right. His children are serving God. His marriage is strong and secure. How wonderful!

Fools on the road have no sense of direction.
The way they walk tells the story: "There goes the
    fool again!"

—*Ecclesiastes 10:3*

Thank God for the people who pray for me because prayer helps keep me on the right path. The right path yields the right results.

Oh folks, we've got to choose the way of wisdom. We've got to walk in the right direction.

If a ruler loses his temper against you, don't panic;
A calm disposition quiets intemperate rage.

—*Ecclesiastes 10:4*

Here the wisdom book of Ecclesiastes is showing us how to live through a negative, angry circumstance, highlighting the concept that we are the key to resolving it. We can choose to stay calm.

YOU MAKE THE CHOICE.

Today, you are making choices. Are you making choices that will bring right results in your life? Or are you making wrong choices then blaming them on everybody else? Wrong choices come from wrong thinking. Wrong thinking comes from not feeding your heart on the Word of God, not having godly friends, and not being accountable to people. Oh, this is so good for you to know, because if you make wise choices, you will enjoy your life so much more! Now let's look and see some more key things about our hearts:

> Here's a piece of bad business I've seen on this
> earth,
> An error that can be blamed on whoever is in
> charge:
> Immaturity is given a place of prominence,
> While maturity is made to take a backseat.
> I've seen unproven upstarts riding in style,
> While experienced veterans are put out to
> pasture.
>
> —*Ecclesiastes 10:5–7*

Sometimes we experience a bad time in life where we feel uncertain about our future through no fault of our own. In these situations, we didn't make a bad choice.

One example is when immature people are chosen for leadership positions. It's hard to know how to handle the situation, especially if it's your boss or one of your children's coaches. Many times we feel we can't speak up about it until the right time.

So what can we do in the meantime? We can pray and we can believe God will turn the negative situation around. Eventually, that immaturity or that ungodliness is going to bring bad results for the immature leader. Then God can turn the situation around, and He can make it work in a new way.

Another example of experiencing uncertainty through no fault of your own is when a person endures a life-threatening illness. I met a pastor's wife who is also a model. Probably in her late forties, she's still stunning. Her hair, skin, eyes, teeth, and figure are gorgeous.

Earlier in life, she won her state's beauty competition, earning her the same "Miss" title as "Miss New York" or "Miss Alabama." She shared with me, "Eight years ago I became ill with cancer and I went through chemotherapy. I lost my hair. I lost my looks. I would look in the mirror and think, *You're a Miss, but you look like you've missed everything.*"

But she continued, "In that timing, I talked to Jesus. He spoke to me and told me He would bring me through and make this work for good in my life. He reminded me of Psalm 138:8 NKJV that says, 'The Lord will perfect that which concerns me.' I answered Him, 'Lord, if I die, I'm going to heaven. If I live, I'm going to trust You and put my confidence in You.'"

Every day, she would remind herself of that scripture

and more. She took the light of God's Word and spoke it.

People said negative, discouraging things to her. Her circumstances said negative things to her. The devil said negative things to her. But today, when you see her, she has no sign of cancer. Her beauty is restored; she has the most gorgeous hair, eyes, and teeth.

Here's something interesting about that lady. The source of her happiness is not in her looks. The source of her happiness is in Jesus and in His Word.

What happened in her time of darkness? She got a hold of God's light that took her through.

How important that is! Get godly wisdom; let God's light shine to dispel the darkness. "The entrance of Your words gives light" (Ps. 119:130 NKJV). Without the entrance of God's Word into your life, you're going to walk in darkness.

You can come up with all kinds of excuses not to read the Bible: "I'm too busy," "I'm in school," or "I have this on my plate." Well then, you're too busy to be bright.

You're going to make stupid decisions if you don't meditate on the Word.

We can make godly choices. We can approach uncertain times with a godly perspective.

Solomon continues to give us more wise advice. Now this is hilarious:

Remember: The duller the ax the harder the work;
Use your head: The more brains, the less muscle.

—*Ecclesiastes 10:10*

In other words, if you're going to go out and do a good job, you're going to have to sharpen up. You're going to have to be cutting edge.

Who would try to cut down a tree with a dull ax, and then wonder why it's taking so long? Sharpen the ax and the job won't take nearly as long. Wisdom tells you to go into a situation sharp and prepared so you'll do better. Have faith *and* prepare yourself to do a good job.

Through the years, women have approached me and said, "Marilyn, you go all over the world. I feel God is leading me to go with you and sing solos in your services."

I have responded, "Well, do you sing solos in your church?"

"No."

"Do you sing in the choir?"

"No."

"Are you taking voice lessons?"

"No."

"Well, I have to tell you no. I don't feel led to take you. You're not sharpening your ax."

People say, "I want to be a great schoolteacher" or "I

want to be a great golfer," but then don't educate themselves or practice enough to overcome their weaknesses and become a success.

Women say, "Oh, I want a husband. I really want to get married." But you are sloppy and fat! You can't cook and you have body odor. Sharpen up, honey! He has eyes, and he can smell. You need to look neat, smell good, and cook well. That way, when a man gets you, he gets a real gift.

I love the next scripture:

If the snake bites before it's been charmed,
What's the point in then sending for the
    charmer?

—*Ecclesiastes 10:11*

What's he saying? Don't get yourself into situations where you can get snake bitten before a person has a chance to get there to help you. In other words, godly advice and godly wisdom help you immensely! One thing godly wisdom advocates is planning ahead—even if you think you can handle a difficult matter, be aware you could fail if you're not on time.

What else does Solomon reveal about foolishness and wisdom?

A wise man's heart *is* at his right hand,
But a fool's heart at his left.

—*Ecclesiastes 10:2 NKJV*

In Solomon's day, the right hand stood for protection. I've gotten into trouble more than once when I've stepped out from under wisdom's protection and allowed my emotions to make foolish decisions for me. God never intended our emotions to lead us.

One day, when Sarah and I were taping a television show, we were appealing for new partners for Marilyn Hickey Ministries. The director approached us and told us what to say.

Sarah and I were caught off guard. We thought our permission should have been asked ahead of time and that we should have had more input into the program. We disagreed with the order of the show.

We found out one of our executive vice presidents had set this order. He explained, "This is what we did last year, and it was very effective. We think you should do the same thing this year."

Everyone could tell it was a little tense on the floor. It was probably more tense in the control room where the executive vice president was conversing with the director.

The director returned and offered, "Well, we thought

you knew what we were going to do because this is what we did last year."

Of course, I'm thinking, *A lot of water has gone under the bridge since last year. I don't remember what we did back then and neither does Sarah.*

But I looked around the room and saw around twelve to fifteen staff members on the floor and up in the control room. It was then I thought, *Sarah and I are about to get into a big argument with an executive vice president? I don't think so!*

God spoke to my heart and said, "It's not just the program at stake. It's you being an example to your staff. You can protest 'You should have done this, and you should have done that,' putting on an emotional show here, or you can be wise."

I made a quick decision to be wise and answered the director, "We'll go with the executive vice president's directions, and if you're not happy with it afterward, then we will even do another program. If they want to change it, we will change it. We'll do whatever is needed here because we are all a part of this together."

Sarah echoed my decision with a hearty, "Absolutely! We have some of our own ideas, but we will do what has been decided is best. We respect our staff and our wonderful team."

We taped the program their way, and they were very excited about how well it came out.

Sometimes we're wrong; our emotions are not always correct. Listening to godly wisdom in a circumstance where we were a leadership example protected us from making a big mistake.

When I arrived home from the taping, I said, "Thank You, Jesus, for keeping me cool at a time when I could have set a very bad example."

We all have emotions. They're wonderful. Through them, we experience joy, happiness, and love! But folks, God didn't intend them to replace the wisdom of God when making decisions. Sometimes you won't feel like doing something, but wisdom will lead you to do it anyway. Wisdom, that right hand, will prevent you from making a foolish emotional choice. You don't want to miss the blessing God gives when you make a wise decision.

The words of a wise person are gracious.
The talk of a fool self-destructs—
He starts out talking nonsense
And ends up spouting insanity and evil.

Fools talk way too much,
Chattering stuff they know nothing about.

—*Ecclesiastes 10:12–14*

How foolish to talk, talk, talk, but never listen. The end result is raving madness. How frightening!

Lucky the land whose king is mature,
Where the princes behave themselves
And don't drink themselves silly.

—Ecclesiastes 10:17

When I was in Jordan, one of our guides revealed a very interesting thing. He said, "The richest thing we have in our country is our king."

I exclaimed, "Really, King Abdullah II?"

"Yes."

"Why do you say that?" I asked.

"Jordan has no oil," he replied. "Saudi Arabia, Yeman, and Oman have lots of oil. But their people don't get the money; only a very small percentage of the top people get it. In our country, we don't have a drop of oil, but we have King Abdullah II. He is causing us to prosper because he loves us all. Our king is the richest thing we have."

That touched me deeply. I thought, Yes, a country can be rich with oil but its people never enjoy it because they don't have the right leadership. And then a country can have no oil, but a king can make right decisions and bless a nation.

In everyday life, we must trust godly wisdom to arise to light our way through the forests of uncertainty. It will even bring us through times of shock and crisis in our lives.

Are you raising a child who is causing you so much stress that you feel absolutely beside yourself? Are you uncertain if he'll ever turn out all right—able to hold down a job, stay married, enjoy healthy friendships?

We have two grown children, Sarah and Michael. We adopted Michael when he was three-and-a-half. From the very beginning he was a problem, and we were very poor at dealing with it. Back then, there were no books instructing people how to raise abused children. All people heard was that environment was the key: If you provided a good environment, then everything would be great.

But that wasn't true. We later discovered that genetic traits and wounds from the past greatly influence the behavior of a child. Since we did not know how to help him effectively, Michael's problems grew.

When he turned eight, I became pregnant with Sarah. When she was born we oohed and aahed over her, and Michael felt left out. We didn't do a good job making him feel included.

In his early teens, Michael got involved in drugs. He would promise us he would stop. We would pray with him. We did everything we knew to do, but he just got worse and worse.

When he was nineteen, we had to ask him to leave our home. This was one of the hardest things I have ever done. Today Michael tells us that was the thing that made him wake up and smell the coffee. With no roof over his head, he began to realize he had to make a turn-around. He was sleeping in Denver's parks where people were being murdered.

I would go to sleep at night sending angels around him to watch over him and keep him (Ps. 91:11) and praying Proverbs 11:21 "the seed of the righteous shall be delivered" (KJV).

Today when I look at Michael, I look at a miracle. He's been delivered from cocaine addiction for perhaps seventeen years. He has a good job. He loves people. I think in our family, he is the most loving and under-standing of us all. He overflows with compassion.

When my husband had knee replacement surgery, Michael came and stayed with him at night for six weeks when I was overseas. They shared a great time of father-and-son bonding. Sarah adores him, and he adores Sarah. Recently, they celebrated her birthday together.

I guess I had a lot of fainting spells during those times with Michael, but I found out that God's Word acts as smelling salts. The Lord revived me often during those times through His Word.

Yes, if you look at this kind of challenge from an under-the-sun perspective, you can feel extremely stressed. If you will let the Son give you His promises for your child from the Bible and if you will welcome the work of the Holy Spirit in your own life, your family can come out smelling like a rose. The bottom line is "in due season we shall reap, if we faint not" (Gal. 6:9 KJV).

All of the things we did wrong and Michael did wrong, God righted. Truly the seed of the righteous is delivered.

chapter 10

adventurous living

What do you do when you have to make a decision and you feel like your back's up against a wall?

This is another part of life, and Solomon shares with you what to do. When you have an opportunity to give, act in faith and do it:

> Be generous: Invest in acts of charity. Charity yields high returns.
> Don't hoard your goods; spread them around.
> Be a blessing to others. This could be your last night.
>
> —*Ecclesiastes 11:1–2*

Many times we must act in faith when we give because we tend to fear we'll run out of what we need for ourselves. Solomon advocates generosity. He says when you give, you're making a decision that causes good things to happen in your life. God notices your generosity and gives generously back to you.

You make the choice. Are you going to be stingy, hindering God from giving to you? Or are you going to be generous so God can overflow in His abundance to you? Then Solomon writes about another faith decision:

> When the clouds are full of water, it rains.
> When the wind blows down a tree, it lies where it
>   falls.
> Don't sit there watching the wind. Do your own
>   work.
> Don't stare at the clouds. Get on with your life.
>
> —*Ecclesiastes 11:3–4*

So what is he saying? Don't let your circumstances measure the good things you desire to do. Don't let them hold you back—I want to invite the youth group over but what if I don't have enough energy to clean my house beforehand? Or what if I give money to a poor family at Christmastime and then discover I can't provide a great Christmas for my own family?

Go ahead and give. Don't wait for the ideal time—that time rarely arrives. Give even if people think you're crazy.

We own a beautiful home in a nice neighborhood of

ten families. Every Christmas, I want to be a witness to my neighbors. For several years, I've taken a gift to them—sometimes I've left something nice in their mailboxes, other times I've given cookies. Over the years, I've come up with different ideas.

For the last two years, I've decorated the outside of our house with beautiful lights. Along with that, I've erected a big sign that reads "Jesus Loves You."

Well that's offensive, you might think.

People may think I'm crazy, but I know this was an idea God laid on my heart. I'm simply obeying Him.

People say, "Take Christ out of Christmas. Let's just make it Happy Holidays." Do you know how the dictionary defines holiday? Holy Day. Consequently, when we say "Happy Holidays" we're saying "Happy Holy Day."

What is Christmas? It's Jesus' birthday. And what's Christmas all about? It's about Jesus' love. He came to Earth to be our Savior. He loved us so much He was willing to come into this world, be tempted in all ways yet never sin, and then die and be raised from the dead where He is now seated at the right hand of the Father today. Christmas is a celebration of our Savior, the only way to the Father.

No one else has died and risen from the dead. No one else lived a perfect life. No one else shed perfect blood for you and me.

We aren't going to act in faith when we're worried about what people are going to think about us.

Solomon continues,

> Go to work in the morning
> and stick to it until evening without watching the
>   clock.
> You never know from moment to moment
> how your work will turn out in the end.
>
> —*Ecclesiastes* 11:6

We don't know when our giving will produce something good. If you give in the morning, it may bring results in the evening. If you give in the evening, it may bring results the next day. Solomon's basically saying, "Give morning and evening."

What happened to a friend of mine will encourage you to become a giver.

One day a friend said to me, "Marilyn, I was reading the scriptures when I realized I needed to make some decisions about how I live. I need to be sure to sow all the time." Even though she had a big financial need of her own, she decided to raise her niece and nephew as her own because their mother was trapped in a drug habit.

When she asked Jesus to come into her life, she helped the children ask Jesus to come into theirs. She took them to church. She and her husband provided for them in their own home, even though it was difficult due to their financial struggle.

People would reprimand her: "You don't have to take care of everybody and his dog. You've already raised your own two children. Why do you have to raise these?"

But she said to me, "Marilyn, no matter what it cost, I felt I had to do it, that God wanted me to do it." She continued, "I'm going to continue to sow in their lives, and I'm going to reap."

Today, her niece and nephew are serving God. The niece has grown into an adult who loves God and is winning people to Jesus as she leads a home-based cell group.

And that's not all. My friend was living a lifestyle of sowing, both morning and evening, doing many inconvenient things for the sake of her niece and nephew. During this season of her life, one day she decided to attend a prayer meeting that we called a mountain-moving prayer meeting.

Here we spoke to our mountains according to Mark 11:23 NKJV which says, "For assuredly, I say to you, whoever says to this mountain, 'Be removed and be cast into the sea,' and does not doubt in his heart, but believes that those things he says will be done, he will have whatever he says." My friend spoke to her mountain of debt, then thanked God for taking care of it. She knew she had sown and that she would reap a harvest.

That same afternoon, a realtor called her and said, "I've heard you're an excellent broker. I have two hundred houses about to go on the market. Will you do the financing?"

What a tremendous breakthrough!

What if she had chosen not to give because it wasn't convenient?

You see, God's calling you to a venture of faith. Let me tell you, faith is an adventure! If you don't choose a faith-filled life, you're going to live under the circumstances and you're going to feel life is futile. You'll become cynical and depressed.

God wants more for you! But it's your choice.

Life's circumstances are unreliable but faith is stable. The only thing that's stable in my life is faith. I don't know what the next hour holds. I don't know what tomorrow holds.

But I know I have faith in God who makes everything work together for good—even the rotten, ugly things—according to Romans 8:26, which says, "We can be so sure that every detail in our lives of love for God is worked into something good."

I can't look at the circumstances. Suddenly a tree can fall. Calamities can come. Keep your faith in God and don't procrastinate by saying, "Well, when it's more convenient, then I'll do it."

Solomon warns us not to live life trying to figure everything out, or we'll be so frustrated we won't be able to stand it!

> Just as you'll never understand
> the mystery of life forming in a pregnant woman,
> So you'll never understand
> the mystery at work in all that God does.
>
> —*Ecclesiastes 11:5*

I have a good friend who shared a story with me about her son. When he was a senior in high school, he rebelled against his parents and ran away from home. He had been raised in a godly household where both parents are born-again, Spirit-filled Christians.

They prayed and he came home, but he came home with a rotten attitude. One day while he worked out at a fitness training center, he whined to a trainer about his parents.

"My parents are Christians and they demand this and they expect that and I'm supposed to be in at such and such a time. They won't even let me drive the car."

The trainer responded, "Did you say your parents are Christians?"

"Yes."

"Have they been divorced from each other?"

"No."

"They love you, provide a home for you, and care about you. Yes, they put restrictions on you. They make you go to church, right? My father was a cocaine addict and ended up in prison. My mother was a prostitute. Why don't you just go home? You're stupid. Tell your parents you're sorry and thank God you have such good parents."

He did it. We'll never understand how God arranges it all, but He does!

Just as you don't know how a child is formed in the womb, you don't know how your miracle is going to come.

Another friend of mine, a striking African-American, has probably the most passionate heart for people who don't know Jesus I've ever seen. She loves to work with prostitutes and drug addicts, and goes out on the inner city streets to tell people about the Lord.

Her church wanted to reach out to inner city residents for a week during Juneteenth, which is the celebration of the slaves being freed. She lined up a park, held meetings, and served food. She thought of all kinds of ways to encourage people to come and hear the Gospel.

She asked, "Marilyn, would you come and preach for me?"

I said, "Oh, I would love to do it."

I preached and gave an altar call. She asked if I would take up an offering, so I did. We collected a small amount of money.

Later I asked her, "Now tell me, how much is this week costing you?"

She answered, " It's costing $27,000."

I knew that was a staggering amount for her inner city church to afford, so I said, "I want to share in this, as well as our church and ministry. Would you want me to write a letter to these African-American pastors asking them if perhaps each church could give $500?

"Well," she said, "let me think about it and pray about it with the other churches."

I went home worried, and then I began to pray about it. Finally, I called her about ten days later.

She said, "Oh, quit worrying. My husband just hit another oil well. We're fine!"

Though the offering we received was little, God had another way to meet the need. My friend didn't fret over it—I was the one who went home and worried and prayed and thought of all kinds of ideas to bring the money in. But God did it. It was a wonderful miracle.

Next, Solomon reminds us that God made life to be enjoyed.

Are you thinking, *He did? What is there to enjoy about*

my life? If you look for Him as you go about your daily tasks, you will find Him doing things for you that make you smile.

Watch for Him. Be suspicious. He's up to something good on your behalf.

> Oh, how sweet the light of day,
> And how wonderful to live in the sunshine!
> Even if you live a long time, don't take a single day
>   for granted.
> Take delight in each light-filled hour.
>
> —*Ecclesiastes 11:7–8*

Take delight in the *hour*, not only in the *day*. Enjoy your life!

Instead of looking at what you don't have, look at what you do have. When I was sick with parasites, my days felt awfully dark and gloomy until the moment I realized how dumb I was to live with those feelings as my constant companions.

This is stupid, I told myself. *There are some things I have that are good. Look, I have the sunshine. I have a husband who loves me. I live in a place where I can see beautiful pine trees growing outside my dining room window.*

The more I thought about it, the more I found to be thankful for! I realized I actually had a whole lot to enjoy! From that moment forward, I wrote a list of "thank-yous" every day. Throughout the day, every time one would occur to me, I would write it down. Before I went to sleep at night, I would read my entire thank-you list. Oh my goodness, I had so much!

God didn't make life to be a drag! If your life is a drag, it's because you're living life under the sun instead of living life under the Son. You can be living life under the sun even if you've asked Jesus to come into your life if you are not watching for His goodness toward you each day. It's there! He's there!

The good news is, watching for God's goodness toward you is a choice you can make. Give yourself permission to enjoy Him, and to enjoy what He's giving you moment by moment.

Are you alive? Say, "Thank You, Lord, that I'm alive. Life is Your gift to me today. Thank You that I'm still here." Do you have a job? "Thank You, Lord, for giving me a job. I'm going to allow myself to feel satisfied with every little thing I do today as I work. You want me to enjoy what I accomplish."

During the times when you enter into His presence with praise where you feel His warmth and love, do you thank Him for the gift of Himself? Are you married? Do you have children? Can you see? Can you taste? "Thank You, Lord! *I enjoy my life in you!*"

While you live here on earth, live thanking God. When you experience dark times, when you're tempted to think life is worthless and all your efforts are going down the drain, remember to watch for God. Thank God. Every day. Moment by moment. Hour by hour.

Watch for God's goodness as you work in your particular workplace—home, airplane, office building, the forest, ocean, hospital, classroom, studio—wherever your kind of work takes you. Every hour has something special in it from Him. Catch Him doing something good for you!

What will happen to your view of life? It will change from focusing on the repetitious, daily boredom of life on earth to focusing on God. You will become a person who recognizes and thanks God for His gifts to you. You will be transformed into a person who believes God is working on your behalf in every season of your life and who gives to others in need. What's more, you'll become a person who realizes that God actually desires for you to enjoy life, which He gave to you! Acknowledging His permission to enjoy it, you will become a person who enjoys life! Then he said,

You who are young, make the most of your youth.
Relish your youthful vigor.

Follow the impulses of your heart.
If something looks good to you, pursue it.
But know also that not just anything goes;
You have to answer to God for every last bit of it.

—*Ecclesiastes 11:9*

Set the course of your life while you're young. Pursue your interests. Do things you enjoy. Just remember to be careful not to engage in harmful things that can hurt you down the road.

Make faith decisions. Having fun with godliness can bring tremendous harvest in your life. Live life as a venture of faith.

Solomon's saying, "Come on board here. Let's be a blessing to others. Let's act in faith. Let's look at each hour and each day in faith. Let's be productive in our youthful years."

Now Solomon identifies some things that can hinder your life of faith:

Therefore remove sorrow from your heart,
And put away evil from your flesh,
For childhood and youth *are* vanity.

—*Ecclesiastes 11:10* NKJV

Sometimes we can be so vexed with our circumstances we would like to slap people sideways. Sometimes our hearts aren't pure and we harbor wrong attitudes. These are things that hinder a life of faith.

A dear friend of mine thought she was going to lose her children to her ex-husband. The two of them were contesting who got the children in court. The judge was very negative toward her, telling her she was going to have to go to jail and she was going to have to pay a lot of back support. The whole situation looked extremely bad for her.

The situation was so vexing to her that she developed a terrible attitude. She thought about killing her ex-husband.

But she came to her senses, realizing that mind-set wasn't going to cut it with the Lord. She decided to forgive her husband and the judge.

Before she appeared in court again, she said, "Marilyn, I probably won't see you for a while because I'm supposed to go to jail." Then she added, "In jail, I'll be a witness."

She went to court. God said to her, "Don't say anything." When her case came up, her husband's attorney argued that she should go to jail.

The judge responded, "You're right, but if she goes to jail she won't be able to work to pay this back support her ex-husband is claiming. Therefore, I don't think that's a good solution."

"Well, then let her go to jail at night, and she can work in the day and pay."

The judge countered, "Well yes, that's a solution but it's not a good one. I think the solution is to just forget the whole thing and let it go."

This very judge who had opposed her changed his mind, allowing her to walk out free!

When she repented of vexation in her head and of the weakness of her flesh—"I'm going to kill him. I'll never forgive"— she began to venture out in faith. She didn't have to say a word in her behalf; God moved in her behalf and gave her a miracle.

Adventurous living is faith-filled living. Tapping into God's wisdom makes our lives enjoyable!

chapter 11

enjoying youth and looking forward to old age

Do you dread old age?

Solomon has plenty to say about it. You may be young and think it's never coming your way.

> Honor and enjoy your Creator while you're still
> young,
> Before the years take their toll and your vigor
> wanes,
> Before your vision dims and the world blurs
> And the winter years keep you close to the fire.
>
> —*Ecclesiastes 12:1–2*

Oh, my goodness! You're going to get old. Maybe you can eat anything now without gaining weight. You can run, ski, and bend down and touch your toes. You can do all these things but old age is approaching.

Solomon describes the way bodies deteriorate. When you read it, you may think, *How depressing!*

> In the day when the keepers of the house tremble,
> And the strong men bow down;
> When the grinders cease because they are few,
> And those that look through the windows grow
>   dim.
>
> —*Ecclesiastes 12:3* NKJV

What are the keepers of your house? Your arms! And the strong men? Your legs.

I have found as people age, especially women, their arms are weak. Men open doors and carry heavy things for us, which contribute to upper-body weakness in women. We begin to lose the strength in our arms and wrists.

As we grow older, our knees weaken. Our legs don't hold us up like they once did. Our eyesight weakens. We can't eat everything we need to eat because we've lost a lot of our teeth.

These are facts and you may not want them, but they're still there.

You can't come and go at will. Things grind to a
   halt.
The hum of the household fades away.
You are wakened now by bird-song.

—*Ecclesiastes 12:4*

We don't hear as well. To some extent, people are probably afraid of falling so they don't get out as much. We don't sleep as well as we used to; we sleep so lightly, even a little bird can wake us up.

What are all the symptoms of old age that Solomon has listed so far? Weak arms. Weak legs. Dim eyesight. Poor hearing. Fewer teeth. Fear of falling.

Wow! It looks bad already, but Solomon continues listing:

Hikes to the mountains are a thing of the past.
Even a stroll down the road has its terrors.
Your hair turns apple-blossom white,
Adorning a fragile and impotent matchstick body.
Yes, you're well on your way to eternal rest,
While your friends make plans for your funeral.

—*Ecclesiastes 12:5*

The elderly experience fright over the thought of a walk down the road because they imagine several ways they can get hurt before they reach home. If that weren't bad enough, hair turns white and sexual desire fades!

It's inevitable that our bodies will age here on earth under the sun. Our bodies will go downhill.

> Remember your Creator before the silver cord is
>   loosed,
> Or the golden bowl is broken,
> Or the pitcher shattered at the fountain,
> Or the wheel broken at the well.
>
> —*Ecclesiastes 12:6* NKJV

In other words, we are going to die. Afterward, it will be too late to make a decision about where we want to go—heaven or hell.

Jesus spoke about heaven and hell. It's wise to ask Him to be our Savior as soon as possible in life, so we experience a more enjoyable existence and are assured a place in heaven the moment we die.

It's better to remember God when we're young before our bodies decay.

Are you thinking, *Thanks a lot. I didn't dread old age before, but now I do.*

Here's the great news—Solomon only described under-the-sun old age. Would you like to know about under-the-Son aging?

First of all, the Bible tells us God is going to give us new bodies when we go to heaven. You'll like this—it's so good: "who will transform our earthly bodies into glorious bodies like his own. He'll make us beautiful and whole" (Phil. 3:21).

But what about our bodies now, here on earth? Do your arms have to weaken? Do your knees have to fail? Does your eyesight have to dim? Do you have to lose your memory? Do you have to become hard of hearing? Do you have to lose all of your energy and strength? Do you have to lose all of your sexual desire?

Christians have a choice. We can live each part of our lives in the Son victoriously, including old age.

Moses did it. God revealed to him that He is Jehovah Rophe meaning "the Lord our health," recorded in Exodus 15:26.

How long did Moses live? One hundred twenty years. Did he lose the strength in his arms? Did he lose the strength in his legs? No—he climbed a mountain right before God took him home to heaven.

Did he lose his eyesight? No—the Bible says his eye was not dim when he was one hundred twenty. Did he lose his hearing? No. Did he lose his memory? No. Did he lose his sexual drive? No, he did not. How did this happen? He knew Jehovah Rophe as His God; not only the Lord his healer but the Lord his health.

Which is better? To have to get healed over and over or to get healed once and stay healthy?

If a person is healthy his entire life, then how does he die? Well, how did Moses die? God took him home.

He could just take you home in a breath. We don't have to depart through the jaws of death. We could exit through the gates of glory if we get a hold of who God is.

Are you saying things about your body that aren't true for a person who knows God? People repeatedly say to me, "I'm getting older and when you get over forty-two, you begin to forget things."

I have not found that in the Bible. Where does it say in the Bible that after forty-two you lose your memory? But I have found 1 Corinthians 1:30 KJV that "God is made unto us wisdom." I have found in the Bible in 1 Corinthians 2:16 KJV that "we have the mind of Christ." It doesn't say the mind of Christ over forty-two is forgetful.

Folks, we are claiming things about life under the sun rather than life in the Son. Jesus has provided benefits for our bodies on earth that we must claim. That's why Solomon keeps urging us to choose to believe.

All right, you say, where does it say that? Do you re-member that Jesus said, "I came so they can have real and eternal life, more and better life than they ever dreamed of" (John 10:10)? That's not just eternal life which is absolutely, superbly wonderful, but that's life right here.

Look at the woman who was caught in adultery and the new life that Jesus gave her (John 8:3). Look at the woman who touched his clothes and her twelve-year bleeding condition stopped (Luke 8:43). Look at the man at the pool of Bethesda who had been lying sick in bed for thirty-eight years until the day Jesus healed him and he stood up and walked again (John 5:9). Tell me these people didn't experience abundant life.

What about John who wrote the book of Revelation? Tell me he didn't have abundant life when, probably in his nineties, he wrote the twenty-two-chapter book of Revelation. And that was only after, according to history, the Romans persecuted him by throwing him in a pot of boiling oil!

But his body wouldn't boil, so they fished him out and exiled him to the island of Patmos. He could have settled for depression, feeling alone and worthless. He could have given up, saying, "I'm old. What's the use?" But he lived and wrote the last book of the Bible.

When I was seventy, I started memorizing the Gospel of John. It took me almost two and a half years, and, at the end, I could recite all twenty-one chapters.

If you want an under-the-Son body, you're going to have to speak to your body, telling it to get in line with the fact that God is your health. And that's not all you can do.

Minds and bodies don't automatically go downhill. It's what you do with your mind that counts. It's what you do with your body that matters.

Is it hard for your arms to lift things? Do your legs feel weak when you stand? Why don't you exercise? Why don't you eat properly?

Why allow your body to deteriorate? God gave us one body and He instructed us to glorify Him in it (1 Cor. 6:19–20). We remember to glorify God in our spirits by praising Him and in our minds by thinking godly thoughts, but forget to honor Him with our bodies.

Many times God has a great plan for us but because we don't take care of our bodies, we don't fulfill His will for us on this earth.

I know a true story about a man who's no longer living. As a young man, he was called of God, anointed of God, and moved in the miraculous. People experienced outstanding healings that many had never heard of before under his ministry.

But he abused his body. In his late thirties or early forties, he would go out after a service and eat steaks and the most fattening foods. He'd stay up until two or three in the morning. He expanded to over three hundred pounds in weight.

Not only that, but he had hurt some pastors who had been a blessing to him, and he wasn't handling money properly.

God told him to deal with these matters. But he didn't and he died suddenly.

He caused his early death by refusing to take care of his body and refusing to believe God for supernatural health. I believe God had perhaps a thirty- or forty-year ministry plan for him.

I think that must have hurt God. He must have thought, *Oh, what a waste. I put so much in you. I trained you. I taught you. Your ministry could have gone to a greater height but you didn't take care of your body and relationships.*

Our souls—minds, will, emotions—influence our willingness to believe God for supernatural bodies. Life under the sun is cynical, critical, and depressing.

Why allow those feelings to dominate your day? Did you know you can encourage yourself?

David encouraged himself when he was down. "Why art you cast down, O my soul? And why are you disquieted within me? Hope in God; For I shall yet praise Him, The help of my countenance and my God" (Ps. 43:5 NKJV).

He was talking to himself: "Soul, trust in the Lord." He encouraged himself by telling his soul to trust God.

Don't be discouraged about your physical condition. My mother had a bad case of osteoporosis. She lived to be around ninety, but she lived with a lot of pain in her back.

When I went to the doctor for a bone scan, he informed me, "You have some osteoporosis in your spine."

I immediately thought, *No! I'm not under a generation curse. I'm under a generation blessing in the Son.*

I did what I could to help myself: I took calcium, exercised, and found a verse in the Bible about strong bones that I spoke over my spine.

Three years later, I returned for another scan.

Amazed, the doctor announced, "I've never seen anything like this. Your spine is osteoporosis-free."

Honoring God by taking care of His temple and speaking God's Word was health to my bones.

Are you talking to your body? Body, quit eating all the food. Body, get on the treadmill. Body, start drinking more water. Mind, start thinking God's thoughts. Soul, quit being depressed. I'm not putting up with this kind of pressure in my life. I believe God's Word that promises me "They shall still bear fruit in old age; They shall be fresh and flourishing" (Ps. 92:14 NKJV). I'm going to enjoy old age.

chapter 12

ultimate wisdom

How does Solomon wrap up Ecclesiastes? Many times, people's last words are their best.

> The words of the wise prod us to live well.
> They're like nails hammered home, holding life
>   together.
> They are given by God, the one Shepherd.

> —*Ecclesiastes 12:11*

God has given us words that are "goads" (NKJV) or prods. Webster's Collegiate Dictionary defines a goad as "something that pains as if by pricking, something that urges or stimulates into action, or a pointed rod used to urge on an animal."

Have you felt Him prodding you as you've read the words of Ecclesiastes? God will tell you things to provoke you to go in the right direction in life. He will challenge you.

Let me tell you, it's not always easy to serve God. It's hard. It's not easy being in the ministry; if you're a wimp, don't go into it. The ministry is not for the weak; the ministry is for the strong. God constantly goads and challenges us, always giving us a little push, a little prod here and there.

Immediately before Saul's conversion, God prodded him with a provoking question: ". . . why are you persecuting Me? . . .It is hard for you to kick against the goads" (Acts 9:4–5 NKJV). God was challenging Saul to turn in the right direction

It's challenging to hear:

live a godly life,
drinking is going to kill you,
pornography can destroy you and your family,
forgive the person who hurt you,
give when you don't have much for yourself, and
live peaceably when you prefer to knock some sense
    into someone.

But those words are goads, and they are so good for us to heed.

Someone was talking to me the other day. He said,

"When I started on this job, the demands were so hard. It was a difficult time for me."

I replied, "Yes, it was. And God placed even greater demands on you. But the benefits you've received—God has blessed your family—are out of this world."

"Well," this person said, "the people who enter the company now don't have those demands."

But they do. Maybe the job doesn't goad them, but God does. Everyone pays the price to live well.

"This generation doesn't work hard." Then this generation won't prosper.

"This generation doesn't have a long attention span." Then this generation isn't going to learn much.

"This generation won't spend time in prayer." Then this generation is not going to experience the supernatural manifestations of God.

You see, God doesn't change His principles with each new generation. His principles remain the same generation after generation. The principles that worked in my generation work in your generation and in the next generation. Truth doesn't change.

Let me tell you, there have been times when I've thought, *Where am I going to go? What am I going to do?* And I have found that God's Word was a nail that was sure and secure. I could hang my life on it. I would not go under if I would obey Him.

I remember the first time I went through a financial crisis. We had a radio ministry, and we were way behind in our bills. The situation looked so dismal we wondered if we should pull off all the radio stations. And I had just begun! We were seventy thousand dollars behind. That was a tremendous amount of money.

I was preaching in New York State and the pastor said to me, "We are starting a Teen Challenge. Would you mind helping to raise the money for it?"

I said, "How much is it?"

"Seventy thousand dollars."

I thought, *Seventy thousand dollars! That's what I need. And you are asking me, God, to raise it for somebody else?*

When I returned to my room, I was very upset with God. God spoke to me and gave me a scripture about how Daniel always worshipped and obeyed God faithfully. And He added, "Even when it doesn't make any sense to you, will you obey Me and trust Me? Will you obey, even when it looks like you won't be delivered by your faith? Will you be faithful if you have to go into the furnace like Daniel did? Will you be faithful to help someone else even if you lose your own ministry?"

That was a prod, so I responded, "OK."

God gave me such great faith for that Teen Challenge! The night we raised money, Teen Challenge received their biggest offering ever.

I remembered the scripture God had given me: "Your God, whom you serve continually, He will deliver you" (Dan. 6:16 NKJV). I had been faithful to serve God in that situation.

When I arrived home, seventy thousand dollars came in. To this day, I don't know how it came or where it all came from, but it came in. God's Word was a nail I could hang my strength and energy on. He delivered me.

Solomon says the words of the wise that prod us to live well "are given by God, the one Shepherd" (Eccles. 12:11). Principles of positive thinking and others that better our lives are good. I'm not against any of them; I like them.

But unless these principles are given by our Good Shepherd who knows what is best for us, they are not going to work on a long-term basis.

We can trust the Word that endures forever, not positive thinking, which might be gone tomorrow.

Jesus identified Himself as our good shepherd (John 10:11). What is a shepherd? A shepherd is someone who takes care of the sheep and wisely guides them through situations:

GOD, my shepherd! I don't need a thing.
You have bedded me down in lush meadows,
    you find me quiet pools to drink from.
True to your word,

you let me catch my breath
and send me in the right direction.

Even when the way goes through
Death Valley,
I'm not afraid
    when you walk at my side.
Your trusty shepherd's crook
    makes me feel secure.

You serve me a six-course dinner
    right in front of my enemies.
You revive my drooping head;
    my cup brims with blessing.

Your beauty and love chase after me
    every day of my life.
I'm back home in the house of GOD
    for the rest of my life.

—Psalm 23

We can trust this kind of God when He nudges us with goads.

But regarding anything beyond this, dear friend, go easy. There's no end to the publishing of books, and constant study wears you out so you're no good for anything else. The last and final word is this:

Fear God.

Do what he tells you.

—Ecclesiastes 12:12–13

You can struggle and struggle in life. But Solomon advises, "Cool it. Relax and have some fun, because here is the essence of life: Fear God. Do what He tells you."

Decide to be wise. Get up every morning and pray, "God, I want to please you. I fear you. I honor you. I respect you. I know the fear of the Lord is the beginning of wisdom."

Wisdom is the goad that will keep you and me heading in the right direction. When we take a detour—when we want to tell somebody off or when we want to hurt someone who hurt us—wisdom will prod us back on the right path.

Solomon concludes:

And that's it. Eventually God will bring everything that we do out into the open and judge it according to its hidden intent, whether it's good or evil.

—Ecclesiastes 12:14

Eventually, it's all going to come out. We may want to push the thought away, but there will be a judgment day for all the world when God will assess what we've done and why we did it. Everything will be exposed, whether good or evil. On that day, God wants the best in you and me to come out in the open. That's why Solomon finishes his tour of life with this one final Holy Spirit-inspired goad.

Choose to live wisely.

chapter 13

enjoy life!

I tried my level best
to penetrate the absurdity of life.
I wanted to get a handle on anything useful we
    mortals might do
during the years we spend on this earth.

—Ecclesiastes 2:3

King Solomon tried many things to find a sense of meaning in life. His conclusion: Fear God and enjoy life.

God placed a built-in need for eternity on the inside of every person—we know there's something more to life than what we see. Solomon searched through every avenue possible and concluded that God satisfies our deepest longing.

Do you want to view your existence through negative, pessimistic eyes, thinking, *Is this all there is?* Or do you want to look at life through the eyes of faith, thinking, *God loves me and wants me to enjoy life?*

Are you going through the seasons of life thinking, *Overeat, get drunk, and throw expensive parties because tomorrow my body drops into the ground?*

Or are you going through your seasons thinking, *Eat, drink, and be merry because God gives me the ability to enjoy life now and for eternity?*

God loves you and longs for you to enjoy life.

Simply:

Ask "Jesus, please come and shine your light into
　　my dark situation today,"
Trust God to do something good in your situation,
Watch for His answers,
Notice His supernatural touch in your day,
Thank Him for all the little things you enjoy,
Believe He makes all things beautiful in their time,
　　and
Look forward to heaven with Jesus!

Every day is a gift. Let's spend it well, expecting God to transform our hearts, our circumstances, and our lives.

This is a great time to live and enjoy life!

bibliography

Eaton, Michael. *Ecclesiastes*. Downers Grove, Illinois: InterVarsity Press, 1983.

International Standard Bible Encyclopedia, Electronic Database: Biblesoft, Inc., 1996, 2003.

Jamieson, Robert, A.R. Fausset and David Brown. *Jamieson, Fausset and Brown Commentary*. Electronic Database: Biblesoft, Inc., 1997, 2003.

Nelson's Illustrated Bible Dictionary. Thomas Nelson Publishers, 1986.

Thank you to Dean Niforatos, for sharing his personal insights and notes on the Book of Ecclesiastes.